I0079874

CALVIN'S DOCTRINE OF
THE KNOWLEDGE OF GOD

διὰ τούτου ἀτενίσωμεν εἰς τὰ ὕψη τῶν οὐρανῶν· διὰ τούτου
ἐνοπτριζόμεθα τὴν ἄμωμον καὶ ὑπερτάτην ὄψιν αὐτοῦ· διὰ
τούτου ἠνεῴχθησαν ἡμῶν οἱ ὀφθαλμοὶ τῆς καρδίας· διὰ τούτου
ἡ ἀσύνετος καὶ ἐσκοτωμένη διάνοια ἡμῶν ἀναθάλλει εἰς τὸ φῶς·
διὰ τούτου ἠθέλησεν ὁ δεσπότης τῆς ἀθανάτου γνώσεως ἡμᾶς
γεύσασθαι.

Clement of Rome: To the Corinthians, § xxxvi.

CALVIN'S DOCTRINE OF
THE KNOWLEDGE OF GOD

BY

T. H. L. PARKER, M.A., B.D. (Camb.)

WIPF & STOCK · Eugene, Oregon

Wipf and Stock Publishers
199 W 8th Ave, Suite 3
Eugene, OR 97401

Calvin's Doctrine of the Knowledge of God
By Parker, T. H. L.
ISBN 13: 978-1-4982-3203-6
Publication date 6/8/2015
Previously published by Wm. B. Eerdmans, 1952

TO
DAVID AND AILSA KNOX

ACKNOWLEDGMENTS

I wish first of all to thank the Reverend Professor T. F. Torrance for his kindness in reading and commenting on this essay in MS. I am also indebted to him in his capacity as Editor of the *Scottish Journal of Theology* (and to his fellow-editor) for allowing me to use *in extenso* two articles which appeared in that Journal in March and December, 1949, under the title of "Calvin's Concept of Revelation".

I must also thank the Librarian and Staff of the City of Rochester Public Library who took great trouble to obtain books for me, culminating in the triumph of fetching, like Aladdin's genie, a book from the Vienna State Library. And Mr. Peck, of the Cambridge University Library kindly kept a *rusticus* supplied with the statutory number of books per term.

I am grateful to the publishers for letting me include as additional matter, an appendix on E. A. Dowey's *The Knowledge of God in Calvin's Theology*.

My wife, by her assistance, lightened the monotonous labour of compiling references and indices, and of proof-reading.

ABBREVIATIONS AND EDITIONS

C.R.-   *Corpus Reformatorum. Ioannis Calvini Opera quae supersunt omnia. Ediderunt Guilielmus Baum, Eduardus Cunitz, Eduardus Reuss. Brunsvigae.* 1863.
      (The volume numbers refer to *Calvini Opera.*)

C.T.S.-   *Calvin Translation Society. Edinburgh.* 1843 ff.
      (The volume numbers, where given, refer in each case to the volumes of the work quoted. There are no volume numbers to the whole edition.)

CONTENTS

PART TWO
THE KNOWLEDGE OF THE REDEEMER

INTRODUCTION

"CANST thou by searching find out God?" demanded Zophar the Naamathite of stricken Job. To this question, the answers, although many, have of necessity been either *Yes* or *No*, uttered in varying degrees of conviction and intensity. Deistic humanism has answered *Yes*, on the basis of man's divine capability. But this answer could never fully satisfy the Christian Church; for if man can, of himself, find out God, what need of Jesus Christ and of the Holy Spirit? Hence the reply of the Christian theologian has always been a more or less definite *No*, from the "No, but ——" of Catholicism and liberal Protestantism to the *Nein!* that thundered from Basel in the year 1934.

Zophar's angry question might be taken as the problem which Calvin set himself to answer in the *Institutio Christianae Religionis*, the first Protestant work on the knowledge of God, and indeed one of the greatest works produced by the Church on this doctrine. The first edition of 1536 had for its self-confessed aim the instruction in the elementary principles of Christianity (hence the title) of those who, although hungering and thirsting after Christ, had no real knowledge of Him; and also the aggressive defence or confession of the "new" teaching before the persecuting secular powers in the person of the King of France. [1] Although the concept of knowledge does not play a large part in this edition, the seed from which shall later grow the form of the other editions is already present, in the first sentence of the first chapter: "The sum of sacred doctrine is contained almost in these two parts: the knowledge of God and of ourselves." [2] From this beginning he goes on to teach, in one paragraph only, what should be known of God: "He is infinite wisdom, righteousness, goodness, mercy, truth, power and life; so that there is no other wisdom, righteousness, goodness, mercy, truth, power and life (Bar. 3; James I). And wherever we perceive any of these things, they are of Him (Prov. 16). Also, all things both in heaven and

[1] C.R. I, p. 9.   [2] C.R. I, p. 27.

earth were created to His glory. . . . In the third place, He is a righteous Judge, sternly punishing those who swerve from His laws and do not entirely perform His will. . . . Fourthly, He is mercy and gentleness, receiving kindly the wretched and poor who flee to His clemency and entrust themselves to His faithfulness".[1] Thereafter, "the knowledge of ourselves" leads him on to the exposition of the Law. The tone of the first edition is predominantly moral when it treats of man's relationship to God.

In the second edition of 1539, however, we are met by a change. In the first place, the scope of the book becomes wider. Although the dedicatory address to Francis I remains almost as in 1536, with but a few alterations, and those mostly stylistic, there is added a *Preface to the Reader*, in which Calvin deprecates the first edition as treating the subject *leviter*, and now declares his aim to be "to prepare and qualify students of theology for the reading of the divine Word, so that they may have an easy introduction to it, and be enabled to proceed in it without any obstruction".[2]   Accordingly, the *Institutio* assumes a more comprehensive character. The first sentence no longer treats of "*summa sacrae doctrinae*," but of "*summa sapientiae nostrae*".[3] The whole plan of the book is altered and greatly expanded from six to seventeen chapters. In particular we must notice that the first sentence has borne fruit, which is not yet fully mature. Now a whole chapter is given to each of the two branches of knowledge: cap. I. *De cognitione Dei;* cap. II. *De cognitione hominis.*

This form was kept, with various additions to the matter in the 1543 ff. and 1550 ff. editions, until the definitive edition of 1559, when once again the book was redrafted. The scope and purpose remain the same, and the large part of the previous editions since 1539 is incorporated. But now the concept of the knowledge of God predominates. The first book deals with the Knowledge of the Creator; the second with the Knowledge of the Redeemer. The missionary oratory of clay and wattles has been expanded into a cathedral.

[1]C.R. I, p. 27.
[2]C.R. I, pp. 255–6.
[3]C.R. I, p. 279. But are we to take *summa* in the same sense as the mediaeval theologians used it as a title for their books, and hold that Calvin "is consciously offering a world outlook, a complete system."? (A. Dakin: *Calvinism*; London, 1941; p. 11.) Surely such a purpose is quite different from what Calvin declared to be his aim. (And what a summary *summa* the 1536 edition makes!)

The chief source for our understanding of Calvin's doctrine of the Knowledge of God is therefore the 1559 *Institutio*, his last word, so to speak, on the subject. Comparison with the earlier editions is sometimes fruitful, as also between the Latin originals and the French translations which Calvin has left us of every edition from 1539 onwards. The 1560 translation of the definitive edition has often been stated to have been badly revised by other translators, but J. W. Marmelstein shows (quite conclusively, to my mind) that it was Calvin's own translation.[1]

The *Institutio* needs also to be compared with Calvin's other writings, and particularly with the Commentaries. There is nothing in the Commentaries that does not also come in the *Institutio*, but at the same time there are a good many things which he expresses far more forcefully and sometimes more fully in them. We could wish that he had given us commentaries on the Wisdom literature. They would have been helpful for our present study! With regard to the Sermons, the position is rather different. They are authoritative, certainly, but they are popular and are concerned to impress upon unlearned people the religious significance of what his text says. I have therefore made very little use of them.

As the *Institutio* was the main source, the plan of this book was decided for it, and we have followed fairly closely the argument of the first two books and some of the third book of the *Institutio*. But a sustained simple exposition of the text of a theologian becomes soon boring to writer and reader alike, and therefore I have tried to recast Calvin's material, by asking his questions and trying to arrive at his answers in company with him. But where I seem to have left my text and argue on my own account, I think it will be found that I have argued "Calvinishly". Certainly the essay must be judged on the grounds as to whether it has faithfully reproduced Calvin's doctrine of the knowledge of God.

[1] J. W. Marmelstein: *Étude comparative des Textes latins et français de l'Institution de la Religion Chréstienne par Jean Calvin.* Groningen, den Haag. 1923. It is a great pity that this extremely important book is not known in England. Even as late as 1946 a writer on Calvin accepted the criticisms of the editors of *Corpus Reformatorum* against the 1560 translation. (R. E. Davies: *The Problem of Authority in the Continental Reformers.* pp. 106–7.) The two most important textual conclusions reached by continental scholars are this of Marmelstein that 1560 is Calvin's own translation, and that by P. Barth and W. Niesel that 1536 also had its own translation—though no copy is known of this, unfortunately.

But, as Bultmann says, "we do not stand outside historical sources as neutral observers; we are ourselves moved by them; and only when we are ready to listen to the *demand* which history makes on us do we understand at all what history is about. This dialogue is no clever exercise of subjectivity on the observer's part, but a real *interrogating* of history, in the course of which the historian puts this subjectivity of his in question, and is ready to listen to history as an authority". [1] This I have tried to do with Calvin; and in doing so, have observed that he is not willing to remain buried in the sixteenth century, but comes forward to carry on a theological discussion in his incisive manner with us to-day.

[1] D. Rudolf Bultmann: *Jesus and the Word.* (London, 1935) p. 4.

Part One
The Knowledge of the Creator

CHAPTER ONE

THE SELF-REVELATION OF THE CREATOR

1

THE CONCEPT OF REVELATION

AT the beginning of the *Institutio* there may be perceived a remarkable omission. The subject of the book is the knowledge of God; but Calvin does not lay the foundation for his building by first proving the existence of the God who is to be known. He does not neglect the problem, but by his treatment of it seems to leave a gap in his argument that, if he were writing from a certain theological viewpoint, would invalidate his conclusions. How different from St. Thomas Aquinas, who, pursuing partly the same aim as Calvin, asks at the outset of the *Summa Theologica*, "whether the existence of God is self-evident": "*Objection* 1. It seems that the existence of God is self-evident. Now those things are said to be self-evident to us, the knowledge of which is naturally implanted in us, as we can see in regard to first principles. But as Damascene says (*De Fid. Orth.* i. 1, 3), the knowledge of God is naturally implanted in all. Therefore the existence of God is self-evident. . . . *Reply Objection* 1. To know that God exists in a general and confused way is implanted in us by nature, inasmuch as God is man's beatitude. For man naturally desires happiness, and what is naturally desired by man must be naturally known to him. This, however, is not to know absolutely that God exists; just as to know that someone is approaching is not the same as to know that Peter is approaching, even though it is Peter who is approaching; for many there are who imagine that man's perfect good which is happiness, consists in riches, and others in pleasures, and others in something else." [1] He therefore feels compelled by the necessity of logical completeness to demonstrate *a posteriori* the existence of God in the famous five proofs.

Calvin, however, presupposes the existence of God, on the very ground, the validity of which St. Thomas denies, that men have an innate knowledge of the existence of God. It is true that

[1] *Summa Theologica.* Qu. II. Art. 1.

this is not to be regarded as *cognitio Dei* but at the most as *notitia Dei* (which two terms he contrasts in *Institutio* i. iii. 3) but it is a real *notitia*. The expressions he uses convey the validity he attaches to it. It is *sensus divinitatis* [1] or *sensus deitatis;* [2] an *impressio de numine;* [3] *constans illa de Deo persuasio* [4] or *ingenita persuasio, esse aliquem Deum;* [5] it is *semen religionis* [6] or *propensio ad religionem;* [7] it is *notio Dei.* [8] In other words, it is a more or less conscious feeling or idea that apart from the world of men there is Another; a feeling or idea that naturally is believed intellectually, and is disbelieved only in defiance of nature, and that naturally finds expression in worship.

This knowledge of the existence of God is innate, and a necessary attribute of man: "this is a doctrine, not first to be learned in the schools, but which every man from his birth is self-taught". [9] This, indeed, and the worship which accompanies it, "is the only thing that makes men superior to the brutes".[10] It is, moreover, indelible. Neither the lapse of time nor the perverted desire of men to be free from God can uproot it from their being: "I only maintain, that while the stupid insensibility which the impious wish to acquire that they may despise God, festers in their minds, yet the sense of a Deity, which they ardently desire to extinguish, is still strong, and frequently shows itself . . . though many strain every nerve to be rid of it, yet nature itself allows none to forget".[11] All men, even atheists, the grossly wicked and the complacent bourgeois, know that there is a God. They may not feel or believe this continually, or perhaps

[1] *Inst.* I. iii. 1. C.R. II, p. 36 (twice). I. iii. 3. C.R. II, p. 37.
[2] *Inst.* I. iii. 3. C.R. II, p. 38.
[3] *Inst.* I. iii. 1. C.R. II, p. 36.
[4] *Inst.* I. iii. 2. C.R. II, p. 37.
[5] *Inst.* I. iii. 3. C.R. II, p. 37.
[6] *Inst.* I. iii. 1. C.R. II, p. 36.
[7] *Inst.* I. iii. 2. C.R. II, p. 37.
[8] *Inst.* I. iii. 2. C.R. II, p. 37.
[9] *Inst.* I. iii. 3. C.R. II, p. 38. Cf. P. S. Watson: *Let God Be God!* (London, 1947), pp. 76 ff. Luther, like Calvin, allows that "even the heathen have this awareness (*sensum*) by a natural instinct, that there is some supreme deity (*numen*). . . . For this knowledge is divinely implanted in the minds of all men . . . even if they afterwards err in this, who that God is and how He wills to be worshipped". (W. A. XLII. p. 631. Quoted by Mr. Watson, p. 80.) The similarity between the two reformers on this matter is striking. Calvin was, in many respects, a better Lutheran than the old quarrel between Lutherans and the Reformed would allow.
[10] *Inst.* I. iii. 3. C.R. II, p. 38.
[11] *Inst.* I. iii. 3. C.R. II, pp. 37-8.

even as frequently as Calvin suggests, but on certain occasions the overpowering sense of the existence of God come upon them inescapably.

Since, therefore, Calvin holds to the reality of this innate knowledge of God, he does not need (even apart from the theological impropriety) to argue the existence of God. Nor does St. Thomas' illustration about the fictitious Peter invalidate Calvin's position at all, for the "five-proofs" do not in fact tell us who God is, but only that He is, together with certain probable facts about His nature which do not in themselves constitute a sufficient object of knowledge when it is nothing less than the knowledge of God with which we are concerned. We know, if you like, that the man who is coming is named Peter, but we do not know this Peter who is coming. The innate knowledge of God tells us as much (and as little, of course) as the demonstrations of the existence of God, for it is the knowledge—hazy, imperfect, half-buried, yet still present—that there is *God*. [1]

With this foundation laid, Calvin is able to continue with his theme of the knowledge of God.

The problem of the knowledge of God is the problem of revelation. This is true, as Brunner has pointed out, [2] of all religions; it is not a principle peculiar to Christianity. It nevertheless becomes particularly significant in respect of Christianity, for then the word revelation receives a certain rigorous interpretation which binds the knowledge of God indissolubly to it in

[1] We must disagree with B. B. Warfield, who, after asserting that Calvin points us to the works of God rather than to the proofs of his existence, yet leaves the door open for them to re-enter into Reformed theology by stressing Calvin's "practical religious motive." The inference presumably is that this motive is purely one of method, and incidental, and that there was a Calvin who allowed a speculative motive and the proofs that go with it. If so, it was not the Calvin whose theological works we have. Although Warfield speaks of Calvin's "special interest in the theistic argument," and says that "He asserts their [i.e. the proofs'] validity most strenuously" (*Calvin and Calvinism* (New York, 1931), p. 41 and n. 8), he does not say where all this activity is to be found. In point of fact, of course, it comes from reading back into Calvin another motive and other thoughts, culled from the course of scholastic Calvinism, which not only are not to be found in Calvin, but also do violence to the motive of his theology. Neither chapter 3 nor chapter 5 of Book I ought to be interpreted as supplying the Calvinian equivalent to St. Thomas' "demonstrations."

[2] "Through God alone can God be known. This is not a specifically Christian principle; on the contrary, it is the principle which is common to all religion and, indeed, to the philosophy of religion as a whole. There is no religion which does not believe itself to be based upon divine revelation in one way or another." E. Brunner: *The Mediator* (Eng. Trans., 1934), p. 21.

that form which is the peculiarity of Christianity. This rigorous interpretation consists in the defining and emphasizing of the identity of God as the subject of revelation and the object of knowledge. That is to say, it consists in the regarding the God who makes Himself known as the only true God, in opposition to all those fictitious gods created by man's hands or mind. The God who reveals Himself in such and such a way is the one God beside whom there are no others. He is, moreover, the God who is known in a way corresponding with this certain revelation of Himself. *"Nec enim arbitratu hominum fingendus est Deus,"* says Calvin in a classic sentence, *"sed ita comprehendendus ut sese nobis declarat."* [1] It is the exclusive interpretation of the Name *God* which gives its significance to the Christian assertion that the problem of the knowledge of God is the problem of revelation. Thus Karl Barth says: "Knowledge of the truly one and only God gains this meaning when it is brought about by this truly one and only God Himself. God is the one and only One and proves Himself to be such by His being both the Author of His own Being and the source of all knowledge of Himself. In both these respects He differs from everything in the world. A God who could be known otherwise than through Himself, i.e. otherwise than through His revelation of Himself, would have already betrayed, *eo ipso*, that He was not the one and only One and so was not God". [2]

Because the problem of the knowledge of God is the problem of revelation, a study of the knowledge of God ought not to begin with an enquiry into the nature of knowledge. Until the concept of revelation has been discussed in respect of its necessity, nature and forms, and the validity of those forms, the concept of knowledge has no meaning as applied to God. Once, however, the problem of revelation has been stated and an answer on the basis of the scriptural witness found, the problem of the knowledge of God has also received its answer fundamentally. When we know what revelation means, we also know what is the knowledge of God. It then becomes possible to consider that knowledge itself—although even then it cannot be considered by itself, but

[1] *In Isai.* 52: 6. C.R. XXXVII, p. 246.
[2] *The Knowledge of God and the Service of God according to the Teaching of the Reformation.* Gifford Lectures, 1937–8. (Translated by J. L. M. Haire and I. Henderson. London 1938.) pp. 19–20.

only in connection with what has been said of the concept of
revelation.

This is Calvin's approach to the problem in the *Institutio*.
When he lays it down as a principle in the first sentence of Book 1
that "nearly the whole sum of our wisdom . . . consists in these
two parts: the knowledge of God and of ourselves," he does not
go on to consider knowledge, but revelation, in the chapters that
follow. Indeed, although the subject of the whole *Institutio* is
the knowledge of God in its various aspects, he does not deal at
all with the knowledge of God in isolation but only with knowledge in the light of revelation.

"Words cannot express, or feeling embrace, or reason apprehend the results of enquiry carried further;" says Hilary of
Poitiers, "all is ineffable, unattainable, incomprehensible". [1] This
declaration of the Divine incomprehensibility is necessary to
Christian theology. But in what does it consist? We are not now
considering the barrier between God and man set up by sin,
since the connection between knowledge and revelation does
not primarily depend upon redemption, for "even had man
remained free from all blemish, his condition was too lowly for
him to reach to God without a Mediator". [2] God is incomprehensible, in the first place, because He transcends man in every
respect: "the Divine nature is infinitely exalted above the comprehension of our understanding". [3] He is incomprehensible, in
the second place, because to have laid Himself open to the
scrutiny of any who cared to investigate His Person would have
been to have surrendered Himself and therefore His freedom and
His sovereignty to the will of His creatures. This the Incarnate
Son could do; and the meaning of His suffering is that He freely
laid aside His freedom and suffered men to do what they would
with Him. But this the Eternal God will not do, for He is always
impassibilis as the Sovereign Lord of men. He retains therefore
the knowledge of Himself as a mystery, a secret known only by
Himself. The idea of *Deus absconditus* is as native to Calvin's
theology as to Luther's, with whom it is generally associated.
"*Quia Deus ipse procul absconditus lateret . . .*" [4] Or: "*Nam quum*

[1] *De Trinitate* II. 5.
[2] *Inst.* II. xii. 1. C.R. II, p. 340.
[3] *In Ps.* 86. 8. C.R. XXXI, p. 794. C.T.S. III, p. 385.
[4] *Inst.* III. ii. 1. C.R. II, p. 398.

sit natura incomprehensibilis, et ab humana intelligentia procul absconditus. . . ." [1] The hiddenness of God plays, indeed, a necessary part in Calvin's doctrine of revelation and in his soteriology. In a passage where Hilary's influence is not confined to the bare quotation, Calvin says: "For how can the infinite essence of God be defined by the narrow capacity of the human mind, which could never yet certainly determine the nature of the body of the sun, though it is the object of our daily contemplation? How can the human mind, by its own efforts, penetrate into an examination of the essence of God, when it is quite ignorant of its own? Wherefore let us freely leave to God the knowledge of Himself. For 'He alone,' as Hilary says, 'is a competent witness to Himself, being known by Himself alone.' And we shall certainly leave it to Him, if our conceptions of Him correspond to the manifestations which He has given us of Himself, and if our inquiries concerning Him are confined to His word". [2]

Even apart from any idea of sin, God is incomprehensible in His transcendence and voluntary hiddenness, and therefore is unknown to man unless He makes Himself known to him. The presupposition of man's knowledge of God is the self-revelation of God; and the presupposition of the self-revelation of God is His incomprehensibility.

Revelation implies not only the impossibility of knowledge without it but also the will of God to be known and His ability to make Himself known, as well as the capability of man to receive revelation (even if this capability is caused by revelation itself). Unless these meanings are given to it, revelation becomes a meaningless word. However we conceive of it, revelation can be no other than a movement from God to man that it may occasion a movement from man to God.

No Christian theologian had ever taught otherwise, indeed, for his theology would *ipso facto* have ceased to be Christian—and that at the very point where the quality of the whole theology as Christian or pagan is decided. Even where man's capabilities are magnified unduly, his movement towards God is still made

---

[1] *Inst.* (1539), cap. I. C.R. I, p. 286.

[2] *Inst.* I. xiii. 21. C.R. II, p. 107. One of the most notable features of Hilary's *De Trinitate* is the reverence that he shows for the mystery of God. His influence in this respect on Calvin is frequently apparent in the Reformer's theology.

dependent upon the prior revelation of God. Thus St. Thomas never dreams of placing God at the disposal of man's intellect in the way that has sometimes been attributed to him: "the created intellect cannot see the essence of God, unless God by His grace unites Himself to the created intellect, as an object made intelligible to it". [1]

The same is true of the more conservative Bonaventure, whose thought is reconstructed by E. Gilson as "God must inform our intellect in order to be known by it;" [2] and also of Duns Scotus: "Thus a being who exists only in virtue of a free decision of God, because it has no necessary relation to God, will know God only in virtue of another divine decision equally free". [3] There are, however, degrees of denial, and it is possible to give a large place to man's capabilities in redemption without denying the priority of God's grace. But Calvin will have none of this. For him man's only rôle is that of beholding the revelation, of hearing the Word, of receiving salvation. The movement is from God right down to man who has not moved a step towards God. Apart from the self-revelation of God, no knowledge of God is possible to man at all. The problem of the knowledge of God is the problem of revelation.

2

THE WORKS OF GOD

Properly speaking, there is (as we shall see in a later chapter) only one revelation of God; that is, the Word of God: "as all Divine revelations are justly entitled *the Word of God*, so we ought chiefly to esteen that substantial Word the source of all revelations, who is liable to no variation, who remains with God perpetually one and the same, and who is God Himself". [4] There is, however, more than one form of the one revelation; and it is to these forms of revelation that we have now to turn. The first

---

[1]*Summa Theologica.* Qu. XII, Art. 4.
[2]E. Gilson: *The Philosophy of St. Bonaventure.* (Eng. Trans. by Dom Illtyd Trethowan and F. J. Sheed, London, 1938), p. 120.
[3]E. Gilson: *The Spirit of Mediaeval Philosophy.* (Eng. Trans. by A. H. C. Downes, London, 1936), p. 256.
[4]*Inst.* I. xiii. 7. C.R. II, p. 95. Cf. *in Gal.* 3:19: "since the beginning of the world God has held no intercourse with men, save through the agency of His eternal wisdom or Son." C.R. I, p. 216. C.T.S., p. 102.

is the *opera Dei*, by which Calvin means all the creative and providential activity of God. "We know God, who is Himself invisible, only through His works." [1] "*Pource qu' il s'est manifesté à nous par ses oeuvres, il faut qu'en icelles nous le cherchions.*" [2]

The conception that has grown up of Calvin as an enemy to all beauty, and a somewhat liverish pilgrim averting his eyes from the loveliness of the world through which he must, unhappily, pass, has only been able to exist where there has been ignorance of his writings. Unfortunately, such ignorance has not always been regarded as incompatible with the understanding of Calvin's thought and with writing books about him. But merely one morning's reading in the *Commentary on Genesis*, or that on the *Psalms*, or Book I, chapter 5 of the *Institutio*, would show us how false is the idea of the Reformer obtaining even among some professional historians and theologians.

Time and again he reverts to the praises of God who created the world not merely useful—that is, a suitable place for man's abode—but also beautiful. "For God—otherwise invisible—(as we have already said) clothes Himself, so to speak, with the image of the world, in which He would present Himself to our contemplation. They who will not deign to behold Him thus magnificently arrayed in the incomparable vesture of the heavens and the earth, afterwards suffer the just punishment of their contempt in their own ravings. Therefore, as soon as the Name of God sounds in our ears, or the thought of Him occurs to our minds, let us also clothe Him with this most beautiful ornament." [3] Or take this: "We see the world with our eyes, we tread the earth with our feet, we touch innumerable kinds of God's works with our hands, we smell the sweet and pleasant fragrance of herbs and flowers, we enjoy boundless benefits; but in those very things of which we attain some knowledge dwells such an immensity of divine power, goodness and wisdom as absorbs all our senses". [4] This hardly sounds like a man hating earthly beauty and despising the handiwork of God. Not Richard Jefferies could have written more feelingly.

But if he praises the beauty and wonders of the earth, he is

---

[1] *Argument to Commentary on Genesis.* C.R. XXIII, p. 7. C.T.S. I, pp. 59–60.
[2] *Le Catéchisme de Genève.* C.R. VI, p. 15.
[3] *Arg. Comm. on Gen.* C.R. XXIII, p. 7. C.T.S. I, pp. 59–60.
[4] Ibid. C.R. XXIII, p. 6. C.T.S. I, pp. 57–58.

still more moved by the majesty of the heavens. "He only makes mention of the heavens; but under this part of creation, which is the noblest and more noticeably excellent, he doubtless includes by synecdoche the whole fabric of the world. There is certainly nothing so obscure or contemptible, even in the smallest corners of the earth, that some marks of the power and wisdom of God may not be seen in them. But as a more distinct image of Him is engraven on the heavens, David has particularly selected them for contemplation, that their splendour might lead us to contemplate all parts of the world. When a man, from beholding and contemplating the heavens, has been brought to acknowledge God, he will learn also to reflect upon and to admire His wisdom and power as displayed on the face of the earth, not only in general, but even in the smallest plants." [1]

We may observe, in this connection, that Calvin, as an educated gentleman (in the days when it was still possible for a gentleman to be educated) was no mere theological specialist. Besides his competence in the humanities, he was obviously interested in the sciences—in medicine, in natural history (sometimes delightfully curious), in astronomy. Particularly in astronomy. (This characteristic attitude of Calvin contemplating with uplifted eyes the stars, is a parable of his religious attitude also—*Sursum corda!*) We find him turning with evident enjoyment to the subject again and again. "How great must have been the Artist who disposed that multitude of stars which adorn the heaven in such a regular order, that it is impossible to imagine anything more beautiful to behold; who fixed some in their stations so that they cannot be moved; who granted to others a freer course, but so that they never travel beyond their appointed limits; who so regulates the movements of all that they measure days and nights, months, years, and seasons of the year; and also reduces the inequality of days, which we constantly witness, to such a medium that it occasions no confusion." [2] "Adepts, indeed, in those liberal arts, or those initiated into them, are thereby enabled to proceed much further in investigating the secrets of Divine wisdom. Yet ignorance of those sciences prevents no man from such a survey of the workmanship of God,

[1] *In Ps.* 19. 1. C.R. XXXI, p. 194. C.T.S. I, pp. 308–9.
[2] *Inst.* I. xiv. 21. C.R. II, pp. 132–3.

as is more than sufficient to excite his admiration of the Divine Architect. In disquisitions concerning the motions of the stars, in fixing their positions, measuring their distances and distinguishing their peculiar properties, there is need of skill, exactness and industry. . . ." [1]

Yet, lovely and magnificent as are the heavens and the earth, there is an even more wonderful example of God's handiwork—man, the crown of the creation. We shall be disappointed if we look for disparagement of man in the pages of Calvin. Man is the "pre-eminent specimen of Divine wisdom, justice and goodness;" [2] "Some of the ancient philosophers have justly called man a microcosm, or world in miniature, because he is an eminent example of the power, goodness and wisdom of God, and contains in him wonders enough to occupy the attention of our minds, if we are not indisposed to such a study". [3] In his soul immortal; in his mind noble; most exquisite in the fashioning of his body.

Thus far we have spoken of the beauty of the creation. So could have spoken any poetic naturalist. The distinctiveness of the Christian doctrine of the creation can be displayed if we compare Calvin with a typical naturalist. Let us choose Richard Jefferies, a most keen observer of nature with a remarkable power of description; a man, moreover, to whom nature spoke with real meaning. Richard Jefferies and Calvin (a seemingly ill-assorted pair) are at one in their admiration for the universe, even though the one experienced the joy of beholding nature a thousand times more intensely than the other. *Wild Life in a Southern County*, with its wealth of detailed and intimate observation, could only be written because what he saw so clearly he felt so intensely. So far Calvin and Jefferies differ only in degree, not in kind. But when they come to the meaning of nature they part company once for all. For Jefferies the desire and delight of life was to be in communion with nature herself and so to experience wholeness, to be in concord with himself and with the world. "I was utterly alone with the sun and the earth. Lying down on the grass, I spoke in my soul to the earth, the

[1] *Inst.* I. v. 2. C.R. II, p. 42.
[2] *In Gen.* I. 26. C.R. XXIII, p. 25. C.T.S. I, p. 92.
[3] *Inst.* I. v. 3. C.R. II, p. 43.

sun, the air, and the distant sea far beyond sight. I thought of the earth's firmness—I felt it bear me up; through the grassy couch there came an influence as if I could feel the great earth speaking to me. I thought of the wandering air—its pureness, which is its beauty; the air touched me and gave me something of itself. I spoke to the sea: though so far, in my mind I saw it, green at the rim of the earth and blue in deeper ocean; I desired to have its strength, its mystery and glory. Then I addressed the sun, desiring the soul equivalent of his light and brilliance, his endurance and unwearied race. I turned to the blue heaven over, gazing into its depth, inhaling its exquisite colour and sweetness. The rich blue of the unattainable flower of the sky drew my soul towards it, and there it rested, for pure colour is rest of heart. By all these I prayed." [1]

For Calvin the creation has no meaning in itself, apart from the Creator. When he admires its beauty, it is the *opera Dei* that he admires. He refuses to accord a self-sufficiency to the universe, and will not be satisfied with the creation, but must let it speak to him of its Author: "We know God, who is Himself invisible, only through His works. . . . This is the reason why the Lord, that He may invite us to the knowledge of Himself, places the fabric of the heaven and earth before our eyes, rendering Himself in a certain manner manifest in them. For His eternal power and Godhead (as Paul says) are there exhibited (Rom. 1. 20). And that declaration of David is most true, that the heavens, though without a tongue, are yet eloquent heralds of the glory of God, and that this most beautiful order of nature silently proclaims His admirable wisdom (Psalm 19. 1). This is the more diligently to be observed, because so few pursue the right method of knowing God, while the greater part adhere to the creatures without any consideration of the Creator Himself. For men are commonly subject to these two extremes: namely, that some, forgetful of God, apply the whole force of their mind to the consideration of nature; and others, overlooking the works of God, aspire with a foolish and insane curiosity to inquire into His essence. Both labour in vain. To be so preoccupied with the investigation of the secrets of nature, as never to turn one's eyes to its Author, is a most perverted study; and to enjoy

[1] *The Story of My Heart* (London, 1907), pp. 4–5.

everything in nature without acknowledging the Author of the benefit is the basest ingratitude". [1]

Not merely, however, does the creation speak to him of God. It is the self-manifestation of God. This he frequently asserts:

"He hath so manifested Himself in the whole workmanship of the world, and daily shows Himself openly, that men cannot open their eyes without being forced to see Him." [2]

"The symmetrical arrangement of the world is like a mirror, in which we may contemplate the otherwise invisible God." [3]

"The world is created for the display of God's glory." [4]

"The Lord clearly represents both Himself and His immortal kingdom in the mirror of His works." [5]

"That we may enjoy the sight of Him, He must come forth to view with His clothing; that is to say, we must cast our eyes upon the very beautiful fabric of the world in which He wishes to be seen by us." [6]

"In the splendour of the heavens there is presented to our view a lively image of God." [7]

In what sense, however, is the creation the revelation of God? It is, as we have already seen, the *opus Dei*, or, more specifically, the *opificium Dei*, which, as such, bears impressed upon it the signs of the workmanship of its *Opifex:* "on each of His works He has inscribed unmistakable marks of His glory". [8] These *certae notae* consist in the beauty, skilful arrangement and usefulness of the creation, which Calvin calls the image of God, or a mirror in which God is to be seen, or the *effigies Dei*. While the three terms are not synonymous, they represent a single well-defined idea in Calvin's theology. The universe is a mirror in which is to be seen the *effigies Dei*, the portrait of God. As such it is the image of God. *Effigies Dei* is equivalent to the *certae notae gloriae suae* which God has inscribed on His workmanship. Thus, in creating the universe God made it a representation of Himself. This He

[1] *Arg. Comm. on Gen.* C.R. XXIII, p. 7. C.T.S. I, p. 59.
[2] *Inst.* I. v. 1. C.R. II, p. 41.
[3] *Inst.* I. v. 1. C.R. II, p. 42.
[4] *Inst.* I. v. 5. C.R. II, p. 45.
[5] *Inst.* I. v. 11. C.R. II, p. 49.
[6] *In Ps.* 104. 1. C.R. XXXII, p. 85. C.T.S. IV, p. 145.
[7] *In Ps.* 19. 1. C.R. XXXI, p. 195. C.T.S. I, p. 309. These quotations could be vastly multiplied from many places in his writings.
[8] *Inst.* I. v. 1. C.R. II, p. 41.

did freely; He need not have left these marks upon His work. For they are not like the adventitious evidences that enable us to "date" or "place" a poem or a concerto. The clues to the period or authorship of a work of art arise from the self-expression of the author, so that even with a parody or a forgery it is possible to ascribe the work to its true author (if he has written anything else). But the *certae notae* are deliberately inscribed by God upon His workmanship for the purpose of making Himself known to men.

Another metaphor that Calvin uses of the creation as revelation is that it is the garment of God, the "visible apparel" of the invisible God: "For God, by other means invisible, (as we have already said) clothes Himself, so to speak, with the image of the world, in which He would present Himself to our contemplation".[1] Luther also uses the same figure, but in a more imaginative manner, as was his nature: "Hence, he who would contemplate such mighty things in safety and without danger, must confine himself with all simplicity within those representations, signs and veils of the Divine Majesty—His Word and His works. For it is in His Word and His works that He discovers Himself unto us; and such as attain unto the knowledge of these are like the woman labouring under the issue of blood—healed by touching these hems of His garment. Those, on the other hand, who strive to reach God without these veils and coverings, attempt to scale heaven without a ladder, that is, without the Word; and in so doing are overwhelmed by the Majesty of God, which they vainly endeavour to comprehend, and fall and perish".[2] Moreover, Luther asserts in a more direct and forcible manner the paradox that God in revealing Himself, conceals Himself: that *Deus revelatus* is *Deus absconditus:* "It is absolutely necessary that when God reveals Himself to us, He should do so under some veil of representation, some shadowing manifestation, and should say, 'Behold, under this veil thou shalt surely discover Me'."[3] This note is hardly sounded by

---

[1]*Arg. Comm. on Gen.* C.R. XXIII, p. 7. C.T.S. I, p. 59.
[2]Luther: *in Gen.* I. 2. W. A. XLII, p. 11.
[3]*In Gen.* I. 2. W. A. XLII, p. 12. For a good exposition of Luther's doctrine of the knowledge of God, both in respect to the creation and to redemption, see G. S. Hendry: *God the Creator* (London, 1937), Chap. 4; and also P. S. Watson: *Let God Be God!* chapters 3, 4, and 5.

Calvin, who, in accordance with his usual direct manner in
theology, considers revelation simply as the making known of
God.   Hence his frequent synonyms for revelation—*fulgere*,
lucere, and their compounds.

The expression *opera Dei* refers not only to the creative
activity of God, but also to His continual providence.   For He
is not only the Creator but the Preserver of all things, and in
His continual ruling of all events both great and small He shows
Himself as God the Creator: "unless we proceed to His providence, we have no correct conception of the meaning of this
article, 'God the Creator'." [1]

The principal passages on the subject in the *Institutio* are three
in number and occur in Book One.   The first (chap. 5, §§
7–8) comes in the context of his exposition on the *opera Dei;*
the second, rather more brief, in chap. 14, § 22; and the third
is the extended essay on the doctrine of providence which ends
the first book (chap. 16–18).   It is, in fact, only an extended
version and detailed defence of the first passage, and therefore
need not occupy us here.

Calvin's concept of God is active, not static.   He attacks the
Epicureans bitterly "who dream of a god absorbed in sloth and
inactivity". [2]   "And, indeed, God asserts His possession of
omnipotence, and claims our acknowledgement of this attribute;
not such as is imagined by sophists, vain, idle and almost
asleep, but vigilant, efficacious, operative, and engaged in
continual action; not a mere general principle of confused motion;
as if he should command a river to flow through the channels once
made for it, but a power constantly exerted on every distinct
and particular movement.   For He is accounted omnipotent, not
because He is able to act, yet sits down in idleness, or continues
by a general instinct the order of nature originally appointed by
Him; but because He governs heaven and earth by His providence, and regulates all things in such a manner that nothing
happens but according to His counsel." [3]   Hence we reach the
conclusion that "nothing can happen but what is subject to His
knowledge and decreed by His will". [4]   All events are the works

[1]*Inst.* I. xvi. 1. C.R. II, p. 144.
[2]*Inst.* I. xvi. 4. C.R. II, p. 148.
[3]*Inst.* I. xvi. 3. C.R. II, p. 146.
[4]*Inst.* I. xvi. 3. C.R. II, p. 147.

of God equally with the creation; and, being the works of God, they are God's revelation of Himself as the Creator. This is the meaning of the sovereignty of God, so characteristic of Calvin in particular and of Reformed theology in general. God is the sovereign, not only in title and honour, but also in fact. It is intolerable to allow Him the title and deny Him the exercise of sovereignty. He reigns supreme over all; over angels, devil, men and all creatures. [1]

For Calvin, history—public and private—is not a confused miscellany of events and actions. Nor, on the other hand, does it show a clear pattern, exhibiting one or other of the urges of the human mind and soul towards better, or at least different, ideals. He readily admits that from the human side the course of events in the world is anything but clear, and likens it to a storm: "When thick clouds obscure the heavens and a violent tempest arises, from the dark mist that is before our eyes and the thunder striking our ears, terror stupefies all our faculties, and all things seem to us to be mingled in confusion". But he continues: "yet during the whole time the heavens remain in the same quiet serenity. So it must be concluded, that while the turbulent state of the world deprives us of our judgment, God, by the pure light of His own righteousness and wisdom, regulates all those commotions in the most exact order and directs them to their proper end". [2] History is the activity of men ruled, whether they will or not, by God, in the midst of conditions occasioned by God. If men would willingly be ruled by God, the course of history would run peacefully and happily; but since the most of men continually rebel against the will of God and so are ruled unwillingly, disturbances occur. Nevertheless, the chaotic condition of the world must not lead us to think that God is unable or unwilling to rule His world and to govern all affairs.

---

[1]Calvin has frequently been most severely criticised for his doctrine of providence. But at this point he was most sure of himself. Admittedly, the philosophical problems raised by his doctrine are formidable. But are not the problems raised by a philosophy that would present a tidy concept of the relationship between God and the world even more formidable from the point of view of a Scriptural theology? Our mind boggles at the thought of all things (evil excepted) being directly due to the will of God. But our faith is dismayed if the Father in whom we would trust is curtailed of His sovereignty, and hence of His ability to act the part of a Father towards us in such a universal way as He has promised.

[2]*Inst.* I. xvii. 1. C.R. II, p. 154.

"First, then, let the readers know that what is called providence describes God, not as idly beholding from heaven the transactions which happen in the world, but as holding the helm of His universe, and regulating all events." [1] The sovereignty of God's will can only be perceived in the course of things by faith. [2]

Providence is the self-manifestation of God the Creator. Worldly events are the activity of God, and that which God does show us what He is—it is by His works that we know Him. Thus in the course of nature God reveals Himself as the Father of all men, caring for them in spite of their sin. For example, "the well regulated successions of summer and winter clearly indicate with what care and benignity God has provided for the necessities of the human family". [3] Or, "there is no man of a mind so dull and stupid but may see, if he will take the trouble to open his eyes, that it is by the wonderful providence of God that horses and oxen yield their service to men, that sheep produce wool to clothe them, and that all sorts of animals supply them with food for their nourishment and support, even from their own flesh. And the more that this dominion is apparent, the more we ought to be affected with a sense of the goodness and grace of our God as often as we either eat food or enjoy any of the other comforts of life". [4] The natural order declares to us the bounty of God: "Although in enriching us with His gifts He gains nothing for Himself, yet He would have the splendour and beauty of His nature manifested in dealing bountifully with us; as if His beauty would be obscured if He ceased to do us good". [5] This bounty shows itself in the active "sustaining, nourishing

[1] Inst. I. xvi. 4. C.R. II, p. 147.
[2] The Psalmist "would have us learn in our contemplations upon the wonderful and mysterious providence of God, to lift our conceptions above ourselves and this world, since it is only a dark and confused view which our earthly minds can take up. It is with the purpose of leading into a proper discovery of the Divine judgments which are not seen in the world, that the Psalmist, in making mention of the majesty of God, would remind us that He does not work according to our ideas, but in a manner corresponding to His eternal Being. We, short-lived creatures that we are, often thwarted in our attempts, embarrassed and interrupted by many intervening difficulties, and too ready to embrace the first opportunity which offers, are accustomed to advance too precipitately; but here we are taught to lift our eyes unto the eternal and unchangeable throne on which God sits, and in wisdom defers the execution of His judgments".— *In Ps.* 92. 8. C.R. XXXII, pp. 13–14. C.T.S. III, p. 500.
[3] *In Ps.* 74. 16. C.R. XXXI, p. 698. C.T.S. III, p. 178.
[4] *In Ps.* 8. 7. C.R. XXXI, pp. 94–5. C.T.S. I, pp. 107–8.
[5] *In Ps.* 90. 17. C.R. XXXI, p. 842. C.T.S. III, p. 476.

and providing for everything that He has made". [1] The delicate balance of interdependence between minerals, vegetables and animals, each relying on the others for sustentation, as well as beauty in colour, form, sound and taste, comes from the bounty of God, thus preserving His world. "Rivers run even through great and desolate wildernesses, where the wild beasts enjoy some blessing of God; and no country is so barren as not to have trees growing here and there, on which birds make the air resound with the melody of their singing. If even those regions where all lies waste and uncultivated furnish manifest tokens of the Divine goodness and power, with what admiration ought we to regard the most abundant supply of all good things, which is to be seen in cultivated and favourable regions? Surely in countries where not only one river flows, or where not only grass grows for the feeding of wild beasts, or where the singing of birds is heard not only from a few trees, but where a manifold and varied abundance of good things everywhere presents itself to our view, our stupidity is more than brutish if our minds, by such manifestations of the goodness of God are not fixed in devout meditation on His glory." [2]

But if the goodness of God is shewn in His kindness to all men, it is far more apparent in His dealings with the Church: "The Psalmist passes next from the more general part of His providence towards mankind at large to His special care over His own Church, adverting to what He had done for the redemption of His chosen people". [3] There must also be included "the evidences of His powers . . . which occur outside the ordinary course of nature". [4] The particulars which he enumerates in the *Institutio* are: the punishment of sinners and the reward of the godly; [5] the overthrow of the proud and the exaltation of the humble; [6] God's mercy to sinners; [7] and His succour for the needy. [8] It is thus that God shows Himself as the Creator in the course of world history and in the daily experiences of every man.

---

[1] *Inst.* I. xvi. I. C.R. II, p. 144.
[2] *In Ps.* 104. 13. C.R. XXXII, p. 89. C.T.S. IV, p. 154.
[3] *In Ps.* 66. 5. C.R. XXXI, p. 612. C.T.S. II, p. 470.
[4] *Inst.* I. v. 7. C.R. II, p. 46.
[5] *Inst.* I. v. 7. C.R. II, p. 46.
[6] *Inst.* I. v. 8. C.R. II, pp. 46–7.
[7] *Inst.* I. v. 7. C.R. II, p. 46.
[8] *Inst.* I. v. 8. C.R. II, p. 47.

We have now seen that Calvin teaches that God, besides giving to man an innate knowledge of Himself, also reveals Himself as the Creator in His works of creation and providence. It is here, however, that we must introduce that "But" which makes him not a natural but a Christian theologian.

CHAPTER TWO

THE FAILURE OF NATURE

THE famous sentence with which the *Institutio* begins occurs first in the 1539 edition: "*Tota fere sapientiae nostrae summa, quae vera demum ac solida sapientia censeri debeat, duabus partibus constat, Dei cognitione et nostri*".[1] This is to be found in a different form at the commencement of the first edition: "*Summa fere sacrae doctrinae duabus his partibus constat: Cognitione Dei ac nostri*". [2] They at once proclaim their author to be writing within the tradition of the historical Church, for these two objects of knowledge had commonly been connected. It also brought him, at first seeming, close to the past and future Catholic doctrine. The comparison that comes to mind at once is with Bossuet, whose treatise *De la connoissance de Dieu et de soi-même*, begins remarkably like the *Institutio: La sagesse consiste à connoître Dieu et à se connoître soi-même. La connoissance de nous-même nous doit élever à la connoissance de Dieu*." [3] He then, in the course of his book, shows what he means by knowing ourselves. Man is composed of soul and body, both of which are wonderful examples of God's creativity and teach us something of the nature of our Creator, for "*Dieu . . . se fait connoître lui-même dans ce bel ouvrage*". [4]

It is true that Calvin speaks (though not at such great length—Bossuet dwells on the matter far more than any theologian need do) of knowing the Workman through His workmanship in man. "Thus it belongs to a man of preëminent skill to examine with the critical exactness of a Galen the connection, symmetry, beauty and use of the various parts of the human body. For its composition is acknowledged by all to be so ingenious as to render its Maker the object of deserved admiration. And therefore some of the ancient philosophers have justly called man a microcosm, or world in miniature, because he is an eminent example of the power, goodness and wisdom of God." [5] When he comes to

---

[1]*Inst.* I. i. 1. C.R. II, p. 31. 1539, cap. 1. C.R. I, p. 279.
[2]1536, cap. 1. C.R. I, p. 27.
[3]*Oeuvres complètes*, ed. F. Lachat (Paris, 1864), vol. XXIII, p. 33.
[4]Ibid, p. 175.
[5]*Inst.* I. v. 2–3. C.R. II, pp. 42–3.

treat of the nature of man, he declares that the meaning of the *imago Dei* was that God "would give a representation of Himself by the characters of resemblance which He would impress upon him". [1]

There the likeness between these two theologians on this matter ends, however, for Calvin is concerned to affirm something that plays a very small part in Bossuet: that the knowledge of ourselves principally means the knowledge of our sin. Writing as if he had his seventeenth-century countryman in mind, he says: "There is much reason in the old adage, which so strongly recommends to man the knowledge of himself. For if it be thought disgraceful to be ignorant of whatever relates to the conduct of human life, ignorance of ourselves is much more shameful, which causes us, in deliberating on important matters, to grope our way in miserable obscurity, or even in total darkness. But in proportion to the usefulness of this precept we ought to be cautious not to make a perverted use of it, as we see some philosophers have done. For while they exhort man to the knowledge of himself, the end they propose is that he may not remain ignorant of his own dignity and excellence; nor do they wish him to contemplate in himself anything but what may swell him with vain confidence, and puff him up with pride. But the knowledge of ourselves consists, first, in considering what was given to us at our creation, and how God sweetly continues His grace towards us, that we may know how excellent had been our nature, if it had remained whole; yet at the same time thinking, that nothing that we have is our own, but is conferred upon us by God for us to hold precariously, so that always we may depend upon Him. Secondly, we should remember our miserable condition since the fall of Adam, the sense of which (all glory and confidence brought low) humiliates and overwhelms us with shame". [2]

Now, this means that what was said in the last chapter concerning the self-revelation of God in His works, has now to be severely qualified by considering the object of revelation and his ability to profit by it. God reveals Himself that He may be known. This is axiomatic. Is God then known by means of a

---

[1] *Inst.* I. xv. 3. C.R. II, p. 137.
[2] *Inst.* II. 1. 1. C.R. II, pp. 175–6.

consideration of the universe and history? Ideally—or, rather, originally—yes. In fact, no. For between the original and the actual stands the Fall, which alters the whole problem of knowledge and revelation. To the knowledge that "God our Maker supports us by His power, governs us by His providence, nourishes us by His goodness and follows us with blessings of every kind" *genuinus naturae ordo* would lead us "*si integer stetisset Adam*".[1] And this conditional phrase, as Karl Barth points out in *Nein!*, is definitive in the understanding of the early chapters (and indeed, of the first book) of the *Institutio*.

Man in his created state of purity was capable of the knowledge of God. True, he did not know Him immediately, but by revelation by the Word in the *opera Dei:* but he was capable of so knowing Him. There existed a harmony between God, the creation and man, so that man perceived God in His image impressed upon the creation and bestowed upon himself. There was not needed a special illumination of the mind, for man's soul and mind was, in virtue of bearing the *imago Dei*, in a condition of illumination, so that he was capable of hearing the Divine voice, of seeing the Divine image. "The primitive condition of man was ennobled with these eminent faculties; he possessed reason, understanding, prudence and judgment, not only for the ruling of his life on earth, but also to enable him to ascend to God and eternal bliss."[2] "In the beginning, the image of God was conspicuous in the light of the mind, the rectitude of the heart, and the soundness of all the parts of our nature."[3]

For such a soul and mind the *opera Dei* were a valid revelation of God—though even so, they were supplementary to the Word of God (Gen. 2. 16–17). But such a soul and mind ceased to exist when Adam fell. The image of God has been corrupted in such a way that God can now be known only by the special, redemptive illumination of the soul by the Word and the Spirit. Man, being out of harmony with God and with His creation, can no longer perceive the revelation of God which is the true meaning of the universe. It is true that Calvin says "that the Divine image was not utterly annihilated and effaced,"[4] but

[1] *Inst.* I. ii. 1. C.R. II, p. 34.
[2] *Inst.* I. xv. 8. C.R. II, p. 142.
[3] *Inst.* I. xv. 4. C.R. II, p. 138.
[4] *Inst.* I. xv. 4. C.R. II, p. 138.

we must not jump to the conclusion that he means by this that man has any righteousness or soundness, for he continually denies it. The *imago Dei* consists "in the light of the mind, the rectitude of the heart and in the soundness of all the parts of our nature". [1] In another place he draws a division between what in man is destroyed by sin and what is only impaired: "the natural talents in man have been corrupted by sin, but of the supernatural ones he has been entirely deprived. For by the latter are intended both the light of faith and righteousness, which would be sufficient for the attainment of a heavenly life and eternal felicity. Therefore, when he revolted from the Divine government, he was at the same time deprived of those supernatural endowments, which had been given him for the hope of eternal salvation . . . Again, soundness of mind and rectitude of heart were also destroyed; and this is the corruption of the natural talents . . . Reason, therefore, by which man distinguishes between good and evil, by which he understands and judges, being a natural talent, could not be totally destroyed, but is partly debilitated, partly vitiated, so that it exhibits nothing but deformity and ruin. . . . So the will, also, being inseparable from the nature of man, is not annihilated; but it is fettered by depraved and inordinate desires, so that it cannot aspire after anything that is good". [2]

When, therefore, Calvin speaks of the *imago Dei* as not totally destroyed and of something of it remaining, he has in mind this distinction. That which remains of the *imago Dei* is the *humanum*, the faculties of reason and will by which man is man and differs from the brutes. He cannot lose these and remain man. But they are terribly wounded by sin, and cannot penetrate to the mystery of the knowledge of God. The relics of the *imago Dei* must not be conceived of as even the faintest glimmer of light in the soul to enable man to perceive the revelation of God in His works. [3] The actual state of man is that he is "despoiled of his

[1] *Inst.* I. xv. 4. C.R. II, p. 138.
[2] *Inst.* II. ii. 12. C.R. II, pp. 195–6.
[3] N. P. Williams thinks he finds an inconsistency in Calvin: "There is one sentence of the *Institutio* which in words denies the idea of total depravity, in connexion with this vexed question of the virtues of pagans, which, he tells us, have been ordained by God *ne hominis naturam in totum vitiosam putemus*, lest we should think that the nature of man is altogether depraved."—(*The Ideas of the Fall and of Original Sin.* (London, 1927), p. 431). If he had looked at the

divine array;" "a miserable ruin;" "an immense mass of deformity;" ignorant, corrupt, impotent, superstitious, obstinate. "With respect to the kingdom of God, and all that relates to the spiritual life, the light of human reason differs little from darkness; for, before it has pointed out the road, it is extinguished; and its power of perception is little else than blindness, for before it has reached its fruition, it is gone. The true principles held by the human mind resemble sparks; but these are choked by the depravity of our nature, before they have been applied to their proper use. All men know, for instance, that there is a God, and that it is our duty to worship Him; but such is the power of sin and ignorance, that from this confused knowledge we pass all at once to an idol, and worship it in the place of God." [1]

In the section on Calvin in his pamphlet, *Nature and Grace*, Dr. Emil Brunner comes into conflict with the metaphor used of Scripture, as a pair of spectacles for weak eyes: "through Scripture the revelation in nature is both clarified and complemented. Scripture serves as a 'lens', i.e. as a magnifying glass for natural revelation". [2] He understands this metaphor to mean that man's spiritual eyesight is not lost but impaired, so that what is needed is not the creation of new sight, but spectacles to help what sight is left. Man can perceive something of God in His works, but to see Him clearly he needs the supplementary assistance of Scripture.

The metaphor occurs twice in the *Institutio*:

"For as persons who are old, or whose eyes are by any means become dim, if you show them the most beautiful book, though they perceive something written, but can scarcely read two words together, yet, by the assistance of spectacles, will begin to read distinctly,—so the Scripture, collecting in our minds the other-

sentence a second time, he would, perhaps, not have misquoted it to make such nonsense of Calvin's theology. It runs thus, in fact: "*Exempla igitur ista monere nos videntur, ne hominis naturam in totum vitiosam putemus.*" (*Inst.* II. iii. 3. C.R. II, p. 211). The governing word is, of course, *videntur*. Calvin's reply is: "The virtues which deceive us by their vain and specious appearance, will be applauded in civil courts and in the common estimation of mankind; but before the celestial tribunal they will possess no value to merit the reward of righteousness." (*Inst.* II. iii. 4. C.R. II, p. 213).

[1]*In Eph.* 4. 17. C.R. LI, p. 204. C.T.S., p. 290.
[2]*Nature and Grace*, in *Natural Theology*, by E. Brunner and K. Barth. (Trans. P. Fraenkel—London, 1946), p. 39.

wise confused notions of Deity, dispels the darkness and gives us a clear view of the true God." [1]

"Lastly, let us remember, that God, who is invisible and whose wisdom, power and justice are incomprehensible, has placed before us the history of Moses, as a mirror which exhibits His lively image. For as eyes, either dim through age or dull through any disease, see nothing distinctly without the assistance of spectacles; so, in our enquiries after God, such is our imbecility, without the guidance of the Scripture we immediately lose our way." [2]

These passages, taken by themselves, can be interpreted in the sense that Dr. Brunner gives to them. If they are so interpreted, however, they do violence to the tenor of Calvin's theology, and such a way of interpretation is, quite apart from theological considerations, unscientific.

We will first examine Calvin's teaching on the innate knowledge of God, and then consider three passages which show how he was accustomed to use his doctrine of the revelation of God in His works.

1. There exists an inherent, universal and indelible *sensus divinitatis*. Such is the tenor of Book I, chapter 3 (see our chapter 1, § 1). In that chapter, be it observed, he speaks of man as he is,

[1]*Inst.* I. vi. 1. C.R. II, p. 53.
[2]*Inst.* I. xiv. 1. C.R. II, p. 117. B. B. Warfield tries to escape from the difficulty ingeniously, by making the spectacles equivalent to Scripture without the illumination of the Holy Spirit. "The spectacles are provided by the Scriptures: the eyes are opened that they may see even through these spectacles, only by the witness of the Spirit in the heart." (*Calvin and Calvinism.* p. 70.) But this, apart from its Zwinglian and un-Calvinian separation of Word and Spirit, is inadmissible, for Calvin's metaphor certainly says that the Scriptures are to sinful man in regard to the knowledge of the Creator, what spectacles are to a *dim*-sighted man. Peter Barth attacks Dr. Brunner on this question: "When Brunner changes this metaphor of Calvin's for one of his own—Christ pierces our cataract so that we can know in all its greatness, 'the first revelation of God in His creation'—then we at once notice one of the not inessential differences between Calvin and Brunner. According to Calvin, the man with the Scriptures as spectacles continually knows and experiences that he needs the spectacles permanently, and that God's revelation in creation becomes dark to him again immediately he wishes to see it without spectacles. Brunner's cataract-pierced man, on the contrary, is himself become a clear-sighted person who, without having to let himself be continually helped, can now, with uplifted eyes, read the Creator and His ordinances in the cosmos; and what he then, in regained independence, reads in the pages of God's revelation in nature becomes to him an important complement to the knowledge of God in Scripture." (*Das Problem der natürlichen Theologie bei Calvin—Theologische Existenz heute.* Heft 18, 1935, pp. 9–10.)

not as he was before the Fall. Even at the end of chapter 4, when he has shown the outcome of this *sensus divinitatis*, he says: "Yet this is a further proof of what I now contend for, that a *deitatis sensum* is naturally engraved in the hearts of men, since necessity extorts a confession of it, even from reprobates themselves. In the time of tranquillity, they facetiously mock God, and with loquacious impertinence derogate from His power. But if any despair weighs them down, it stimulates them to seek Him, and dictates short prayers; which proves that they are not altogether ignorant of God, but that what ought to have appeared before had been suppressed by obstinacy".[1] In this chapter, however, he shows what is the validity for salvation of the *cognitio insita* and to what its efficacy amounts. The former of these two points is dealt with without more ado in the first three sentences. It has no validity for salvation, since it is either smothered or abused. There is, indeed, sown in the heart of every man a *divinitus religionis semen*, as seed is sown in the womb, but scarcely anyone keeps alive what is conceived in him and in no man does it grow and come to a perfect birth.[2] What happens to it is that it is either at once stifled, or in the rare cases when it is taken seriously, it leads blind man astray: "some perhaps grow vain in their own superstitions, while others revolt from God with intentional wickedness; but all degenerate from the true knowledge of Him. *Ita sit ut nulla in mundo recta maneat pietas.*"[3]

When the seed of religion is cherished man is not led by it to the true worship of God, but into superstition or idolatry. Some think that worship paid to any god is good. Not so, for then what is worshipped is not the true God, but the phantasy of human imagination. We must worship God, not as we imagine Him to be, but as He shows Himself to be. In this lies the abuse of the *sensus divinitatis*. When followed, it leads us to worship. If we were to worship the God who reveals Himself in His works as the Creator, our worship would be good and acceptable to Him. But in no case do we do so. Moved by this innate

---

[1] *Inst.* I. iv. 4. C.R. II, p. 41.
[2] So I interpret the words *ita vix centesimus quisque reperitur qui conceptum in suo corde foveat, nullus autem in quo maturescat: tantum abest ut fructus appareat suo tempore* (*Inst.* I. iv. 1. C.R. II, p. 38).
[3] *Inst.* I. iv. 1. C.R. II, p. 38.

feeling to worship, we worship what we conceive in our minds to be God, whether we call it God the Creator or make some material idol to represent it. Our abuse of the *sensus divinitatis*, therefore, leads us further into sin and away from God.

Or the *sensus deitatis* may be stifled by wickedness. When men desire to follow their own will, whether moderately or into any excess whither it may lead them, they do so in opposition to a constituent part of their own nature. They smother the doubt or the shame that their innate knowledge of God provokes in them; and the more they oppose it, and with the more flagrant wickedness, the more easily do they overcome it. But they can never utterly eradicate it. They are never quite safe from this God-engendered feeling of God, which may leap upon them unexpectedly. In the normal course of their lives, however, they manage to stifle the *sensus divinitatis* and so to forget God. Their life is a denial of the existence of God, for they act as if God did not see their actions and condemn them. On the rare occasions when they are forced to acknowledge God, it is no credit to them. They should worship God voluntarily and joyfully; instead, they have to be forced—by adverse circumstances, perhaps, or by fear—into remembering God.

Therefore, even if the *divinitus religionis semen* is kept alive, it only results in a religion quite different from that which Calvin describes in chapter 2, consisting of faith, fear, reverence and a worship acceptable to God. The child that sinful man brings forth is "a false and vain shadow of religion, scarcely worthy even to be called its shadow". [1] "*Manet tamen semen illud quod revelli a radice nullo modo potest, aliquam esse divinitatem: sed ipsum adeo corruptum, ut non nisi pessimos ex se fructus producat.*" [2]

2. *Institutio* I. v. 11-15. Calvin has been discussing in the earlier part of this chapter the revelation of God in His works. When he has finished speaking of the providence of God and thus has completed his account of the revelation, he at once goes on to say: "But notwithstanding the clear representations given by God in the mirror of His works, both of Himself and of His everlasting dominion, such is our stupidity, that, always inattentive to these obvious testimonies, we derive no advantage

[1] *Inst.* I. iv. 4. C.R. II, p. 40.
[2] *Inst.* I. iv. 4. C.R. II, p. 41.

from them". [1] The most men, when they contemplate the creation, do not go further and consider the Creator, but are content with His works. It is also the general opinion that the world is ruled "by the blind temerity of fortune" rather than by God. Even if God's works turn our thoughts to something beyond them, we think, not of the true God, but of an idol invented by our imagination. However different may be the way men consider these matters "we perfectly agree in a universal departure from the one true God to preposterous trifles". [2] From this source has come all the superstition and ignorance shown not only by the common unthinking multitude, but even by the profoundest thinkers. The sum of it all is "that men, who are taught only by nature, have no certain, sound or distinct knowledge, but are confined to confused principles; so that they worship an unknown God". [3]

This last point, "that they worship an unknown God", he elaborates in the following section: "Now, it must be also maintained, that those who adulterate pure religion (which must necessarily be the case with all who are influenced by their own imagination) are guilty of a departure from the one God. They will profess, indeed, a different intention; but what they intend, or what they persuade themselves, is of little importance; since the Holy Spirit pronounces all to be apostates who, in the darkness of their minds, substitute demons in the place of God. For this reason Paul declares the Ephesians to have been without God, till they had learned from the Gospel the worship of the true God. Nor should this be restricted to one nation only, since in another place he asserts of men in general that they became vain in their imaginations, after the majesty of the Creator had been revealed to them in the structure of the world. And therefore the Scripture, to make room for the only true God, condemns as false and lying whatever was formerly worshipped among the Gentiles, and leaves no God but in Mount Sion, where flourished the peculiar knowledge of God". [4]

In these three sections Calvin has been, as it were, building

[1] *Inst.* I. v. 11. C.R. II, p. 49.
[2] *Inst.* I. v. 11. C.R. II, p. 49.
[3] *Inst.* I. v. 12. C.R. II, p. 50.
[4] *Inst.* I. v. 13. C.R. II, pp. 50–51.

up his case, piling effect upon effect. Now we reach the climax, which must destroy any attempt to make him into a natural theologian: "Vain, therefore, is the light afforded us in the formation of the world to illustrate the glory of its Author, which, though its rays be diffused all around us, is insufficient to conduct us into the right way. Some sparks, indeed, are kindled, but smothered before they have emitted any great degree of light. Wherefore the Apostle, in the place before cited, says, 'By faith we understand that the worlds were framed by the Word of God'; thus intimating, that the invisible God was represented by such visible things, yet that we have no eyes to discern Him, unless they be illuminated through faith by an internal revelation of God."[1]

Has the revelation through the *opera Dei* no validity or even purpose towards us? Yes, but the purely negative one of depriving us of any excuse for sin: "But whatever deficiency of natural ability prevents us from attaining the pure and clear knowledge of God, yet since that deficiency arises from our own fault we are left without any excuse".[2]

3. *Commentary on Psalm* 19. 1–9. The Psalm is in two parts, says Calvin; in the first "David celebrates the glory of God as manifested in His works; and in the other, exalts and magnifies the knowledge of God which shines more clearly in His Word."[3] Although the Psalmist mentions only the heavens, he means to include the whole universe in them. But the heavens are so superlatively magnificent that they are more likely to strike the imagination of a man and make him think of his Creator; after which "he will learn also to reflect upon and to admire His wisdom and power as displayed in the face of the earth".[4] The heavens are not merely a "lively image of God" presented to our view, but preachers declaring the glory of God. This they do "by openly bearing testimony that they have not been constructed by chance, but were wonderfully created by the supreme Architect".[5] "As soon as we acknowledge God to be the supreme Architect, who has erected the beautiful fabric of the universe,

---

[1]*Inst.* I. v. 14. C.R. II, pp. 51–2.
[2]*Inst.* I. v. 15. C.R. II, p. 52.
[3]C.R. XXXI, p. 194. C.T.S. I, p. 308.
[4]C.R. XXXI, p. 194. C.T.S. I, pp. 308–9.
[5]C.R. XXXI, p. 195. C.T.S. I, p. 309.

our minds must necessarily be ravished with wonder at His infinite goodness, wisdom and power." [1]

In the next few pages Calvin, following his text closely as always, elaborates and gives further examples of what he has already said. "David, therefore, with the highest reason, declares that although God should not speak a single word to men, yet the orderly and useful succession of days and nights eloquently proclaims the glory of God, and that there is now left to men no pretext for ignorance; for, since the days and nights perform towards us so well and so carefully the office of teachers, we may acquire, if we are duly attentive, a sufficient amount of knowledge under their tuition." [2]   Moreover, the heavens preach in a language universally understood: "Different nations differ from each other as to language; but the heavens have a common language to teach all men without distinction; nor is there anything but their own carelessness to hinder even those who are most strange to each other, and who live in the most distant parts of the world, from profiting, as it were, at the mouth of the same teacher". [3]   Their language is, of course, not oral but visible: "the language of which mention has been made before is, as I may term it, a visible language, in other words, language which addresses itself to the sight; for it is to the eyes of men that the heavens speak, not to their ears". [4]   And above all he stresses that this revelation is clear: "the glory of God is not written in small obscure letters, but richly engraven in large and bright characters, which all men may read, and read with the greatest ease". [5]

So far, this is the teaching on the revelation in the *opera Dei* with which we are familiar from our first chapter.   But Calvin now turns to the second part of the Psalm, on the Law of God, and at once qualifies everything that he has previously said, by straitly limiting the knowledge to be gained from the *opera Dei* by man in his actual state of sinfulness.   Although the universe does show forth God's glory, man is too blind to see it.   "While the heavens bear witness concerning God, their testimony does

[1] C.R. XXXI, p. 195. C.T.S. I, p. 309.
[2] C.R. XXXI, p. 196. C.T.S. I, p. 311.
[3] C.R. XXXI, p. 196. C.T.S. I, p. 312.
[4] C.R. XXXI, p. 197. C.T.S. I, p. 313.
[5] C.R. XXXI, p. 197. C.T.S. I, p. 313.

not lead men so far as that thereby they learn truly to fear Him
and acquire a well-grounded knowledge of Him; it serves only to
render them inexcusable. It is doubtless true that, if we were not
very dull and stupid, the signatures and proofs of deity which are
to be found on the theatre of the world, are abundant enough to
incite us to acknowledge and reverence God; but as, although
surrounded with so clear a light, we are nevertheless blind, this
splendid representation of the glory of God, without the aid of
the Word, would profit us nothing, although it should be to us
as a loud and distinct proclamation sounding in our ears." [1] In
this strain he comments on the rest of the passage.

4. *Commentary on Romans* 1. 18–23. This is the passage
which Calvin usually takes as his model when dealing with the
revelation of the Creator.

Ver. 19. *Because that which may be known of God is manifest in
them: for God hath shewed it unto them.* This he takes as referring
to the *cognitio Dei insita* of *Institutio* I. iii–iv, and the *cognitio Dei
acquisita* of I. v. "And he said, *in them*, rather than *to them*, for
the sake of greater emphasis; for though the Apostle everywhere
adopts Hebrew phrases, and ב , *beth*, is often redundant in that
language, yet he seems here to have intended to indicate a
manifestation, by which they might be so closely pressed, that
they could not evade it; for everyone of us undoubtedly finds it
to be engraven on his own heart. By saying, that God has made
it manifest, he means that man was created to be a spectator of
this formed world, and that eyes were given him that he might,
by looking on so beautiful a picture, be led up to the Author
Himself." [2]

He develops this in verse 20: *For the invisible things of Him
from the creation of the world are plainly seen, being understood by
the things that are made, even His eternal power and Godhead; so
that they are without excuse.* "God is in Himself invisible; but as
His majesty shines forth in His works and in His creatures
everywhere, men ought in these to acknowledge Him, for they
clearly set forth their Maker. And for this reason the Apostle in
his Epistle to the Hebrews says that this world is a mirror, or the
representation of invisible things. He does not mention all the

[1] C.R. XXXI, p. 199. C.T.S. I, p. 317.
[2] C.R. XLIX, p. 23. C.T.S., pp. 69–70.

particulars which may be thought to belong to God; but he states that we can arrive at the knowledge of His eternal power and Godhead; for He who is the framer of all things, must necessarily be without beginning and from Himself. When we arrive at this point, the Godhead becomes known to us, which cannot exist except accompanied by all the attributes of God, since they are all included under that idea.

"*So that they are inexcusable.* It hence clearly appears what the consequence is of having this evidence—that men cannot allege anything before God's tribunal for the purpose of showing that they are not justly condemned. Yet let this difference be remembered, that the manifestation of God, by which He makes His glory known in His creation, is, with regard to the light itself, sufficiently clear; but that on account of our blindness, it is not found to be sufficient. We are not, however, so blind that we can plead our ignorance as an excuse for our perversity." [1]

The degree of knowledge which men actually attain through the *opera Dei* is "that there is some God" [2]—so he interprets "*For when they knew God.*" They do not apprehend "His eternity, power, wisdom, goodness, truth, righteousness and mercy". [3] Without these attributes He is not God, but an empty phantom; and they, not willing to be taught by God what He is, prefer to follow their own imaginations, and so end in ignorance: "having forsaken the truth of God, they turned to the vanity of their own reason, all the acuteness of which fades and passes away like vapour. And thus their foolish mind, being involved in darkness, could understand nothing aright, but was carried away headlong, in various ways, into errors and delusions". [4]

These three passages follow a common pattern, which may also be seen in a number of other places in his writings—as often, in fact, as he deals at any length with the *opera Dei* as revelation. There is no doubt at all that it represents Calvin's general theological intention, by which we must interpret individual passages. Dr. Brunner is at fault in that he has com-

[1] C.R. XLIX, p. 24. C.T.S., pp. 70–71.
[2] C.R. XLIX, p. 24. C.T.S., p. 71.
[3] C.R. XLIX, p. 24. C.T.S., p. 71.
[4] C.R. XLIX, p. 25. C.T.S., pp. 72–3.

mitted precisely this error of interpreting the whole by a part, and this leads him to interpret the part wrongly in its turn. In particular, he presses the metaphor of spectacles to a use that Calvin did not intend and which is quite foreign to the whole meaning of his theology. We may rather reconstruct his thought thus:

Man was created in a state of harmony with God, with the universe in which he lived and of which he was a part, and with himself. There was no need (to transfer Jeremiah's words to this situation) to teach "every man his neighbour and every man his brother, saying, Know the Lord; for they shall all know me, from the least of them unto the greatest of them, saith the Lord".[1] The knowledge of God was written in man's heart and upon all God's workmanship. But when man sinned, that harmony was shattered, and he became out of fellowship with God, a perplexed stranger in an insecure and dangerous world, and *Mensch in Widerspruch*, man in contradiction with himself, to quote the title of the book by Dr. Brunner. He saw, indeed, that the universe meant something, but he lacked the insight and sympathy with God and with the universe itself necessary to interpret its meaning, and therefore, moved by that inward impulse to knowledge which Aristotle says we all possess, he misinterpreted it. To have interpreted the creation, history and experience aright would have brought him to the knowledge of the Creator. To misinterpret them means that, following his inextinguishable desire for something outside and above himself, he deifies the result of his misinterpretation and worships not the Creator but those idols which he thus conceives. In the whole process he has not risen above himself or his world to God.

The revelation in creation and providence, however, does not cease to be revelation because man does not profit by it. Or rather we may say,—for there is a weakness in Calvin's thought here, though his meaning is clearly this,—that the *opera Dei* are subjectively but not objectively revelation. Theoretically, the revelation fulfils a positive function. God gives all men the opportunity of knowing Him, by manifesting Himself in His works: "As the summit of the *beata vita* consists in the knowledge of God, in order that no man might be precluded from bliss, God

[1] Jeremiah 31:34.

hath not only sown in men's minds the seed of religion already
mentioned, but hath manifested Himself. . . ."[1] Man could
know God thus, if he were not blinded by sin. It is necessary to
stress this point. For no good is done by minimising man's
theoretical possibilities or the reality of the revelation in the
opera Dei. God clearly shows Himself daily to every man. Yet
such is our blindness that no man sees Him.

The conclusion is that man is inexcusable for not knowing
God. And the greater the possibility, the more inexcusable.
The function of the *opera Dei* as revelation is therefore negative,
to take away any excuse for sin and so to make men guilty
before God. As such, it serves as a preparation—also negative—
for the Gospel. In itself it has only this negative function but in
relation to the Scriptures it has a positive function.

In the Scriptures God not only gives a clue to the right understanding of His works, but provides that understanding fully. In
the Scriptures God reveals Himself as the Creator. That is to say,
in His Word God interprets His works. The Scriptures teach us
the meaning and right use of the creation and history, which
otherwise we misunderstand and misuse. Thus the *oracula Dei*
(as Calvin was fond of calling the Scriptures) are necessary to the
understanding of the *opera Dei*. The Biblical revelation of the
Creator does not abolish or even supersede the former revelation.
Nor does it supplement it in the sense that it makes more clear
to man something of which he had a dim perception before. But
it does supplement it in that it is necessary for the clarification
of that which merely perplexed, for the interpretation of that
which was so mysterious that man never understood it at all.
Calvin tells us, on the basis of the Biblical witness, that the
faculty of perceiving the Creator in His works is not merely
impaired, but lost; that man is not suffering from bad eyesight,
but from total blindness.

"A God whom I myself could know," says Dr. Brunner
finely, "to whom I myself could give His name, whom I myself
could think, is not really God. God's proper name can be
pronounced and imparted only by Himself . . . He is the One
whose name, whose existence, cannot be known from anything
else. The God whom we should know from the world, the God

[1]*Inst.* I. v. 1. C.R. II, p. 41.

whom we should find in the depths of our soul or mind, would not be Himself; the freedom, the sovereignty, the lordship of God over the world cannot be known from the world; and the lordship and freedom of God over against us cannot be known from the depths of our mind. The real God, who has His own proper name, is the One who is known only by His telling us His own name". [1]

[1] *The Word and the World*, (London, 1932), pp. 29–30.

CHAPTER THREE

KNOWLEDGE THROUGH THE WORD

THE section on the *opera Dei* by themselves ends with chapter 5 of the *Institutio*, and the whole of the rest of the first book is concerned with the knowledge of God the Creator that is received through the Scriptures. In it, Calvin deals with the nature of the Word of God and its function, the God who is thus known, and the relationship between the Scriptures and the *opera Dei*. The other subjects which come into consideration do so only in connection with these main subjects.

"God alone is a sufficient witness concerning Himself." [1] We must not imagine that we can know God unless He reveals Himself to us. Since the one revelation, however, is frustrated by our blindness, it remains for God, in His grace, to give another that shall be sufficiently bright to pierce that blindness—or rather, that shall, with the revelation it sets before us, give us also the eyes to behold both it and the former revelation as well. "Though the light which presents itself to all eyes, both in heaven and on earth, is more than sufficient to deprive the ingratitude of men of every excuse . . . yet we need another and better assistance, properly to direct us to the Creator of the world. Therefore, He hath not unnecessarily added the light of His Word, to make Himself known unto salvation, and hath honoured with this privilege those whom He intended to unite in a more close and familiar connection with Himself." [2] Thus we are directed to the Holy Scriptures as the source of all our knowledge of God. Without them our search for God will merely be a wandering in a labyrinth of which we do not possess the plan, and in which there is no possibility of our striking upon the right way by accident. Without the teaching of the Scriptures the god whom we worship will be, not the true God, but a product of our own mind, the deification of a projection of our own personality.

In the Scriptures God bears the "sufficient witness to Himself", and He "does not manifest Himself to men otherwise than

[1] *Inst.* I. xi. i. C.R. II, p. 74.
[2] *Inst.* I. vi. i. C.R. II, p. 53.

D

through the Word". [1] Therefore it is with the Scriptures that we
must begin if we are to know and worship God our Creator:
"This, then, must be considered as a fixed principle, that, in
order to enjoy the light of true religion, we ought to begin with
teaching from heaven; and that no man can have the least taste
of pure and wholesome teaching save him who will be a disciple
of Scripture". [2]   And again: "For what is the beginning of true
learning but a ready promptness to hear the Word of God?" [3]

1

THE NATURE AND FUNCTION OF THE SCRIPTURES

The Scriptures are the Word of God by virtue of their origin
and by virtue of the ever-living and ever-fresh quickening of the
Holy Spirit. Thus they are the Word of God because the Holy
Spirit spoke them once and speaks them again. So that the
expression "the Holy Spirit says" is synonymous in Calvin for
"the Scripture says". This Divine authorship cannot, however,
be proved by any natural process, and indeed ought not to
be so proved, for such proof would provide a natural instead of a
supernatural foundation for faith, which would therefore cease
to be a supernatural and transcendent quality and become
merely a human faculty. It would, in effect, destroy faith in the
God who speaks in Scripture by destroying faith in the Word
which He speaks.

In answer to the question, "Who can assure us that God is
the Author of the Scriptures?" Calvin replies that the Scriptures
themselves so assure us.   They are self-authenticating—
αὐτοπίστον. But when he speaks of Scripture he joins to it
the Holy Spirit by an unbreakable bond. As we have said, the
Scripture is the Word of God because it has been spoken by the
Spirit, who, moreover, continues to speak that same Word. The
self-authentication of the Scriptures, therefore, does not rest,
as Calvin himself tries to make it rest in Book I, chapter 8, on
certain qualities of the Bible considered as a book, but upon the
Scripture as the living and quickening Word of God. He is

[1]*In Gen.* 3: 6. C.R. XXIII, p. 60. C.T.S. I, p. 153.
[2]*Inst.* I. vi. 2. C.R. II, p. 54.
[3]*Inst.* I. vii. 5. C.R. II, p. 60.

using a dangerously two-edged weapon when he sets out his "Rational Proofs to Confirm Belief in the Scripture". [1] "The majesty of the Spirit is everywhere evident," [2] he tells us. Perhaps; but this is not a rational proof, but belongs rather to the previous chapter on the testimony of the Holy Spirit. "The antiquity of Scripture" [3] is as historically valueless to-day as it was theologically valueless in 1559. And so we might continue through the nine or ten proofs he brings forward. Some are certainly more weighty than others; but strong or weak, they collectively constitute a blemish on Calvin's doctrine of the Word of God which has had for its progeny the busyness of fundamentalists to prove the truth of the Bible to the neglect of discovering and preaching the Truth of the Bible.

The self-authentication of the Scripture rests upon its function as the living Word of God. The same Holy Spirit who spoke that Word formerly, speaks it to us again creatively, giving us ears to hear, a mind to understand, and a heart to believe. We may thus go further, and say that the self-authentication of the Scriptures is the *testimonium Spiritus Sancti*. We follow the Scriptures because we *believe* that God is their Author. "Let it be considered an undeniable truth, then, that they who have been inwardly taught by the Spirit, feel an entire acquiescence in the Scripture, and that it is αὐτοπίστον, carrying with it its own evidence, and ought not to be made the subject of demonstration and rational arguments; but it obtains the credit with us which it deserves by the testimony of the Spirit." [4] In answering the question, "Who can assure us that God is the author of them?" Calvin has also answered the question "Why is the Bible alone given this position in the Church?" The Bible, he says, is not given this position by the Church; rather, it takes it of its own accord, and all the Church can do is to accept this authority over herself obediently. Since she is convinced, with "a sentiment that cannot

[1] Title of *Inst.* I. viii.
[2] *Inst.* I. viii. 2. C.R. II, p. 62.
[3] *Inst.* I. viii. 3. C.R. II, pp. 62–3.
[4] *Inst.* I. vii. 5. C.R. II, p. 60. We may|underline this idea by quoting from the section called *The Written Word of God* in Karl Barth's *Dogmatik*—a section which, when compared with the relevant chapters in the *Institutio*, both interprets the earlier work and also is enlightened by it: "The statement, 'The Bible is God's Word,' is a confession of faith, a statement made by the faith that hears God Himself speak in the human word of the Bible." *Kirchliche Dogmatik.* I. 1, p. 112. (Eng. Trans. by G. T. Thomson (Edinburgh, 1936), p. 123.

be produced but by a revelation from heaven" [1] that the Scripture is the Word of God, she cannot do otherwise than obey it—i.e. regard it as her Lord, because as the Word of her Lord it is the presence of her Lord with her. "Wherefore, when the Church receives it, and seals it with her suffrage, she does not authenticate a thing otherwise dubious or controvertible; but, knowing it to be the truth of her God, she performs a duty of piety, by treating it with immediate veneration." [2]

The title of chapter six, following, it is important to notice, upon the chapter in which the self-revelation of God in His works is discussed and found insufficient, runs thus: "*Ut ad Deum creatorem quis perveniat, opus esse Scriptura duce et magistra.*" *Scriptura duce et magistra* (the same phrase occurs in the *Commentary on Genesis* [3]) is at once Calvin's statement of policy in the *Institutio* and the basis of his doctrine of the knowledge of God. How do we know God? As He has revealed Himself to us in the Scriptures. In obedience to God's Word is the foundation—*Timor Dei initium sapientiae*—and the growth of knowledge. "How can the human mind, by its own efforts, penetrate into an examination of the essence of God, when it is totally ignorant of its own? Wherefore, let us freely leave to God the knowledge of Himself. For 'He alone,' as Hilary says, 'is a competent witness to Himself, being only known by Himself.' And we shall certainly leave it to Him, if our conceptions of Him correspond to the manifestations which He has given us of Himself, and our enquiries concerning Him are confined to His Word . . . [We should] not allow ourselves to investigate God anywhere but in His sacred Word, or to form any ideas of Him but such as are agreeable to His Word, or to speak anything concerning Him but what is derived from the same Word." [4]

Here we have a classic statement of what is technically called the "formal principle" of the Reformation: that the Bible alone is the norm and criterion for thought and life. Calvin's own theological work was carried out in loyalty to this principle. The man who laboured to interpret the Scriptures in commentary and preaching to his contemporaries regarded himself as ruled

[1] *Inst* I. vii. 5. C.R. II, p. 60.
[2] *Inst*. I. vii. 2. C.R. II, p. 57.
[3] C.R. XXIII, p. 53.
[4] *Inst*. I. xiii. 21. C.R. II, pp. 107–8.

by this everliving voice of God. In the *Institutio* as in all his other writings his submission to the Scriptures is clear; the book is a monument to the "formal principle"—or, as Peter Barth very finely said: "*Die Institutio ist gleichsam Calvins Zeigefinger, der auf die Schrift hinweist.*—The *Institutio* is as it were Calvin's forefinger, pointing to the Scriptures". [1] But the "formal principle" of the sovereignty of Scripture as the Word of God is not merely the basis of right theological thinking; it is the basis of the knowledge of the one God. Or rather, we should say that these two were not separate things for Calvin. Right theological thinking was a part of the knowledge of God; the latter being unthinkable apart from the former. It is the fashion in certain circles to-day to decry orthodoxy, under whatever form it appears. In so far as orthodoxy has often, though by no means generally, been accompanied by spiritual sterility, the reaction against it has not been without value. But to decry the right thinking about God which orthodoxy is, is precisely similar to decrying godliness of life. It is true that we should not regard the Bible as a collection of dogmas; and we can go far in sympathising with John Oman when he wrote: "For many, however, the very idea of revelation is the imposition of information and injunction. Then some accept it implicitly for what they take to be the faith, and others reject it utterly for what they take to be freedom. But have we faith except won in freedom, or freedom unless maintained by faith?" [2] The issue is not, however, so clear-cut as Dr. Brunner would suggest in the first chapter of *Revelation and Reason.* To do so he has to dispense with a clear line of thought in the New Testament, where emphasis is laid on "sound teaching". Revelation is not only "the acts of God", not only given in events, not only, as Temple said, given in persons; [3] it is also given in words, the words of Scripture and the words of the preacher. And these words must, if they are to impart to us some idea about God, be words that shall correspond with the truth about God. They shall be words of right theological thinking.

[1] In *De l'Élection Éternelle de Dieu*, p. 242. (Report of the International Calvinist Congress, 1936).

[2] *Honest Religion*. (London, 1941), p. 103.

[3] "Personality can only reveal itself in persons".—*Nature, Man and God.* (London, 1934), p. 266.

The importance Calvin attaches to "sound teaching" is well known. But we must observe that he does so because faith is for him not only an action of the "affections" but of the intellect also; an obedience or assent of the mind as well as obedience of the heart. "They have something on which they may safely rest, when they know that to believe the Gospel is nothing else than to assent to the truths which God has revealed. Meanwhile, we learn that it is peculiar to faith to rely on God and to be confirmed by His words; for there can be no assent unless God has, first of all, come forward and spoken. By this doctrine faith is not only distinguished from all human inventions, but likewise from doubtful and wavering opinions; for it must correspond to the truth of God which is free from all doubt; and therefore, as God cannot lie, it would be absurd that faith should waver." [1] Therefore he can say with such decision: "Would you then be reckoned as belonging to Christ's flock? Would you remain in His fold? Do not deviate a nail's breadth from purity of doctrine". [2]

With this in mind, we turn to Calvin's conception of the function of the Scriptures in respect of our knowledge of God—that is to say, the knowledge of God the Creator. The function of the Scriptures is to teach us who the God is who has created and sustains the universe. Or rather, since the problem stated thus suggests that, starting from a consideration of the universe we come with our questions to the Scriptures, we must follow Calvin more precisely: "God is revealed to us in Scripture as the Creator of the world". [3] This is a frankly didactic view of Scripture: "we ought to learn from Scripture how God, who created the world, may with certainty be distinguished from the whole multitude of fictitious deities". [4] In the Bible is a certain doctrine of God, a line of teaching about God's relationship with the universe. This teaching, because it is God's disclosure of what He has done and continues to do, is the self-revelation of God. The Biblical doctrine of the Creator is the revelation of God. The Biblical doctrine of the Creator is the revelation of the Creator. Therefore, he regards the Scriptures as a school, the

[1] *In Joann.* 3.33. C.R. XLVII, p. 73. C.T.S. I, p. 138.
[2] *In Col.* 2. 8. C.R. LII, p. 103. C.T.S., p. 180.
[3] *Inst.* I. vi. 1. C.R. II, p. 54.
[4] *Inst.* I. vi. 1. C.R. II, p. 54.

Holy Spirit as the schoolmaster and believers as the pupils. [1] If we would know God, we must become the scholars of Scripture.

This leads to a distinctive feature in Calvin's thought. Our sin consists in pride, pride not only of will, but of mind: we are "high-minded". Although we are ignorant, we think we know and that we do not need to be taught like the dunces' table in the village school. But we must humble ourselves to the realization of our ignorance and submit ourselves to the Scriptures. So long as we think we know, we continue in ignorance: "If ye were blind, ye should have no sin: but now ye say, We see, therefore your sin remaineth". [2] It is this abdication of reason from its sovereignty, this *timor Dei*, this obedient submission to the infallible master, that is the foundation of the knowledge of God. "No man can have the least knowledge of true and sound doctrine, without having been a disciple of Scripture. Hence originates all true wisdom, when we embrace with reverence the testimony which God hath been pleased therein to deliver concerning Himself. For obedience is the source, not only of an absolutely perfect and complete faith, but of all right knowledge of God." [3]

This obedience means, in practice, ascertaining what the Scriptures teach and then holding fast to it. It means making the Scriptures the *regula cogitandi et loquendi:* "we should seek in the Scriptures a sure rule both of thinking and of speaking; by which we may regulate all the thoughts of our minds, and all the words of our mouths". [4] And conversely: "let us remember to observe one rule of modesty and sobriety; which is, not to speak, or think, or even desire to know, concerning obscure subjects, anything beyond the information given us in the divine Word". [5]

But it is the obedience of faith, and faith presupposes the illumination of the Holy Spirit. Calvin's doctrine is rescued from regarding the Bible as a sort of school-book setting out the facts to be learned, by the fact that he refuses to think of the Word without the Spirit and because he pays good heed to Hebrews

[1]Zwingli had already used this image before Calvin: e.g. *"Gott will allein selbs der schülmeister seyn."* (*Werke*, Zürich 1828 ff, I, p. 80.)
[2]*John* 9. 41.
[3]*Inst*. I. vi. 2. C.R. II, pp. 54–5.
[4]*Inst*. I. xiii. 3. C.R. II, p. 91.
[5]*Inst*. I. xiv. 4. C.R. II, p. 120.

11. 3: "Through faith we understand that the worlds were framed by the word of God." To understand that the world was created by God we need the teaching of the Bible and the enlightenment of the Holy Spirit. Doctrine becomes revelation at the quickening touch of the Spirit. "Since, then, we are told here that men are unfit to contemplate the arrangements of divine Providence until they obtain wisdom elsewhere than from themselves, how can we attain to wisdom but by submissively receiving what God teaches us both by His Word and by His Holy Spirit? David, by the word *sanctuary*, alludes to the external manner of teaching, which God had appointed among His ancient people; but along with the Word he comprehends the secret illumination of the Holy Spirit." [1] To *believe* that the worlds were framed by God means to be taught from the Scriptures by the Holy Spirit (and therefore inwardly) that God is the Creator and Preserver of the "things which do appear". God reveals Himself in the Scriptures as the true God, the Creator.

2

ORACULA DEI ET OPERA DEI

We have seen that Calvin denies the efficacy of the works of God as a primary source of the knowledge of God, and asserts the sufficiency of the Scriptures for that purpose. From the Scriptures we learn to know God the Creator—that is, we learn His identity and His nature; both, in relation to ourselves. In teaching us this, the Scriptures interpret aright the creation and history: "We must come, I say, to the Word, which contains a just and lively description of God as He appears in His works, when these works are estimated, not according to our depraved judgment, but by the rule of eternal truth". [2] The Scripture is a thread, guiding us through the labyrinth, the enigma of the universe in which we live. The revelation which was frustrated by man's blindness, becomes objectively as well as subjectively,

[1] *In Ps.* 73. 16. C.R. XXXI, p. 682. C.T.S. III, pp. 142–3.
[2] *Inst.* I. vi. 3. C.R. II, p. 55.

revelation by the illumination of the Holy Spirit. The universe is now perceived to be, not an unmeaning or accidental system, but the *opus Dei*. World-history and personal experience of life is no longer regarded tragically, comically or satirically as a chaotic or cosmic sequence of events, but as the *opera Dei*. The Creator, executing His eternal purpose by His sovereign power, upholds and orders all things. That revelation which our sin vitiated into a condemnation, the Word of God restores to a source of knowledge of the Creator. If we begin with the Scriptures and learn to know God from them, we find that the same thing is said by God in His works. "Yet let us not disdain to receive a pious delight from the works of God, which everywhere present themselves to view in this very beautiful theatre of the world. For this, as I have elsewhere observed, though not the principal, is yet, in the order of nature, the first lesson of faith, to remember that, whithersoever we turn our eyes, all the things which we behold are the works of God; and at the same time to consider, with godly meditation, for what end God created them. Therefore, to apprehend by a true faith what it is to our benefit to know concerning God, we must first of all understand the history of the creation of the world, as it is briefly related by Moses, and afterwards more copiously illustrated by holy men, particularly by Basil and Ambrose." [1]

We must stress that, for Calvin, the *opera Dei* were a legitimate and valid means of the knowledge of God—if they were correctly interpreted by the Scriptures. More than that, he held that it is our duty to learn of God by meditating upon the creation and providence. The creation (and not, as Gregory taught, images) is the book of the unlearned. [2] This is, indeed, the proper business of the whole life, in which men should daily exercise themselves, to consider the infinite goodness, justice, power and wisdom of God in this magnificent theatre of heaven and earth. [3] "And it is undoubtedly the will of the Lord, that we should be continually employed in this holy meditation; that, while we contemplate in all the creatures, as in so many mirrors, the infinite riches of His wisdom, justice, goodness and power, we

---

[1] *Inst.* I. xiv. 20. C.R. II, p. 131.
[2] *In Gen.* I. 6. C.R. XXIII, p. 18. C.T.S. I, p. 80.
[3] *In Gen.* 2. 3. C.R. XXIII, p. 33. C.T.S. I, pp. 105–6.

might take not only a transient and cursory view of them, but might long dwell on the idea, seriously and faithfully revolve it in our minds, and frequently recall it to our memory." [1] But we shall not exhaust the Divine significance of the creation quickly, or indeed, at all. The contemplation of the *opera Dei* is a life-long study: "however diligently a man may set himself to meditate upon the works of God, he can only attain to the extremities or borders of them. Although, then, so great a height be far above our reach, we must nevertheless endeavour, as much as in us lies, to approach it more and more by continual advances; as we see also the hand of God stretched forth to disclose to us, so far as it is expedient, those wonders which we are unable of ourselves to discover". [2]

Here we encounter a difficulty. Is not Calvin, by allowing the *opera Dei* to be a medium of the knowledge of God, violating his own cherished principle of *Scriptura sola?* If the Scriptures contain all that is necessary for the knowledge of God, why does he exhort us to the contemplation of the works of God? There is an interdependence between the *oracula Dei* and the *opera Dei*, with the primacy given decisively to the Word of God. The universe is a dark mystery to us unless the *lumen verbi* shines upon it. For this reason the formal principle of *Scriptura sola* is not violated. The Scriptures are indispensable to the interpretation of the mystery of the universe. They are the spectacles which we need to wear to transform chaos into cosmos, things and accidents into the *opera Dei;* and as often as we lay them aside cosmos returns to chaos, *opera Dei* to things and happenings. There is not the slightest question of the *opera Dei* being an independent source of knowledge; or even of them competing with the *oracula Dei* as revelation. Nevertheless if the Word of God is indispensable, so are also the creation and history, for the very obvious reason that they exist alongside us and invite our scrutiny. To neglect them would be to neglect also the Scriptures, where we learn the meaning of them. To contemplate them is not to depart from Scripture, but on the contrary to be obedient to Scripture. The works of God, perceived to be the revelation of God the Creator, do not render the corresponding

---

[1] *Inst.* I. xiv. 21. C.R. II, p. 132.
[2] *In Ps.* 40. 6. C.R. XXXI, p. 409. C.T.S. II, p. 97.

revelation in the Scriptures superfluous, but confirm it. "*Adeo talem sentimus, experientia magistra Deum, qualem se verbo declarat.*" [1]

The Word that reveals the Creator, although it is a "new" Word to us, one which we do not know previous to hearing it and whose content we could never discover for ourselves, is yet not a foreigner in the world, but comes, even as when the Word was made flesh, to its own. There is a real sense in which the Word is always foreign. But this arises, not from its own nature, but from the Fall. To the *imago Dei* the Word is not foreign; but to the sinner it comes as something utterly strange and contradictory to himself. But the Word is in agreement with the *imago Dei* borne by the works of God, and says precisely what they also say. The *oracula Dei* both confirm the *opera Dei* and in turn are confirmed by them.

When by the light of Scripture we come to consider the universe, we find that, although there are many things which we cannot understand and many which distress us, yet it acquires a new meaning. We and our world have a Creator; this Creator is our loving Father; this loving Father is the sovereign Lord, who "reigneth, be the people never so unpatient". By the beauty of the universe, by the fair fruits of man's culture, by good hap—and also by bad—we are pointed to God the Creator. "Finally, to conclude, whenever we call God the Creator of heaven and earth, let us at the same time reflect that the dispensation of all those things which He has made is in His own power, and that we are His children, whom He has received into His charge and custody, to be supported and educated; so that we may expect every blessing from Him alone, and cherish a certain hope that He will never suffer us to want those things which are necessary to our well-being, that our hope may depend upon no other; that whatever we need or desire, our prayers may be directed to Him, and that, from whatever quarter we receive any advantage, we may acknowledge it to be His benefit, and confess it with thanksgiving; that, being allured with such great sweetness of goodness and beneficence, we may study to love and worship Him with all our hearts." [2]

[1]*Inst.* I. x. 2. C.R. II, p. 73.
[2]*Inst.* I. xiv. 22. C.R. II, pp. 133–4.

3

GOD THE CREATOR

What is it to know the Creator, and what is the extent of such knowledge?

The *essentia* of God is and remains incomprehensible to us, for every revelation is under a form. God clothes Himself with a form that He may be seen and known. Yet, that He clothes Himself means that He also hides Himself by that which He puts on, as the nakedness of a man is hidden by his clothes. The very act of revelation entails the accompanying act of veiling and concealing. Hence the *essentia Dei* is always hidden from us. "His essence, indeed, is incomprehensible, so that His majesty is not to be perceived by the human senses; but on all His works He hath inscribed His glory." [1]

It is the glory of God which is revealed in the *opera Dei*,—in the creation; [2] in man; [3] in the angels; [4] and in providence. [5] *Gloria* and *essentia* are opposed to one another in the above quotation, where God's *gloria* is revealed and His *essentia* hidden. For Calvin, *gloria* is close kin to *maiestas;* and it may be taken as the Godhood of God, which separates him from all other beings and differentiates Him from all man-made gods, and which He guards jealously. That God reveals His glory means: God reveals Himself as *God*. Commenting on Isaiah 40. 5, Calvin paraphrases "And the glory of the Lord shall be revealed" as "*maiestatemque suam ac potentiam conspicuam reddat*". [6] And on John 17. 5 he again equates the two words: "*The glory which I had with thee before the world was.* He now declares that He desires nothing that does not strictly belong to Him, but only that He may appear in the flesh such as He was before the creation of the world. Or, to speak more plainly, that the Divine majesty, which He had always possessed, may now be illustriously dis-

---

[1] *Inst.* I. v. 1. C.R. II, p. 41.
[2] *Vide e.g. Inst.* I. v. 1. C.R. II, p. 41; *Inst.* I. v. 5. C.R. II, p. 45; *Inst.* I. v. 15. C.R. II, p. 52.
[3] *Vide e.g. Inst.* I. xv. 3. C.R. II, p. 136; *Inst.* I. xv. 4. C.R. II, p. 138.
[4] *Vide e.g. Inst.* I. xiv. 5. C.R. II, p. 121.
[5] *Vide e.g. Inst.* I. xvii. 1. C.R. II, p. 154.
[6] C.R. XXXVII, p. 9. C.T.S.

played in the person of the Mediator and in that human flesh with which He was clothed".[1]

Majesty, however, is an abstract term, and cannot be seen or known in itself. We perceive majesty when we perceive the exercise of majesty. It is thus that we see God's glory. This Divine exercise of glory is called by Calvin *virtutes Dei*. The word is not easy to define. It properly means powers or excellencies, and is commonly used in the Vulgate to translate δύναμις. Calvin uses the singular as a synonym for *potentia*, but the plural has a different and special signification in his vocabulary. A comparison between the Latin and French texts of the *Institutio* throws considerable light on the meaning. *Virtutes* in the 1539 and 1559 editions is usually translated (by Calvin himself, of course), by its French equivalent *vertus* in the 1541 and 1560 editions, thus leaving the meaning still uncertain. There are, however, two illuminating exceptions.

1. 1539 and 1559 both have: "*A suis enim virtutibus manifestatur Dominus*".[2] The last French edition still has *vertus*: "*Car Dieu nous est manifesté par ses vertus*".[3] This he has altered from the earlier French translations, where he uses *oeuvres*: "*Car Dieu nous est manifesté par ses oeuvres*".[4]

2. "But to avoid the necessity of quoting many passages, let us content ourselves at present with referring to one psalm (Ps. 145), *in quo tam exacte summa omnium eius virtutem recensetur, ut nihil omissum videri queat*."[5] (1539 *and* 1559.) The French remains unaltered from 1541 to 1560: "*Afin que nous ne soyons point contraints d'accumuler beaucoup de passages, pour le présent un Pseaume nous suffira (Ps. 145), auquel toute la somme de ses proprietez est si diligemment recitée, qu'il n'y a rien laissé derriere*".[6]

Now let us see if a common idea arises from this brief comparison of texts. We are presented with three words: *virtutes* or *vertus*; *oeuvres; proprietez*. Both the context and the proper meaning of *virtutes* forbid us regarding *oeuvres* as meaning *opera*

[1]C.R. XLVII, p. 378. C.T.S. II, p. 169. Other examples of this equation of *gloria* with *maiestas* may be found in his writings.
[2]*Inst.* I. v. 9. C.R. II, p. 47. 1539 Ed. C.R. I, p. 289.
[3]*Inst.* I .v. 9. Fr. Ed. 1560. C.R. III, p. 71.
[4]C.R. III, p. 71 n.
[5]*Inst.* I. x. 2. C.R. II, p. 73. 1539 Ed. C.R. I, p. 304.
[6]C.R. III, p. 116.

Dei in the sense in which we are used to the expression in Calvin—as that which God has done or does. It should rather be taken as the act of God working, the activity of God. *Proprietez* does not refer to God's attributes as they are within Himself. Both Psalm 145 and Calvin's commentary upon it, [1] shew that he meant rather the exercise of God's attributes towards men. This is, in fact, no other than the activity of God, *les oeuvres de Dieu.* We can, then, best express *virtutes*= *oeuvres*=*proprietez* as the exercise towards mankind of the attributes of the nature of God.

We are now in a position to take a comprehensive view of the content of the revelation with which the first book of the *Institutio* is concerned.

God reveals Himself to us for His glory and for our salvation; and hence He reveals, not His *essentia* which no man can see and live, but His *gloria* and His *virtutes;* i.e. that He is God and that He will be God towards us. [2] He gives us "a description, not of what He is in Himself, but of what He is towards us, that our knowledge of Him may consist rather in a lively perception, than in vain and aery speculation". [3] But God does not reveal Himself as different from what He is in Himself. He who is revealed is He who reveals Himself. In His revelation we know God and not another. Yet we do not know all about God, for there remains the ultimate which we cannot approach. We know God truly, but we do not know Him wholly. Taught by Scripture, we perceive Him in His works as the Creator. We perceive, that is, His *sapientia, potentia, bonitas, veritas, clementia et severitas,* His *misericordia* and *iudicium,* and His *iustitia.* These are the *virtutes Dei,* which we know from Scripture and the *opera Dei.* They are the content of the revelation of the Creator. To know the Creator is to know Him as the One who exercises towards us His wisdom, power, goodness, etc. We can understand why Calvin says that from the *opera Dei* we know the hands and feet, but not the heart of God. [4]

[1] C.R. XXXII., pp. 412 ff. C.T.S. V., pp. 271 ff.
[2] Cf. K. Barth: "*Darum sind alle seine Vollkommenheiten Vollkommenheiten seiner Liebe.*" *Die kirchliche Dogmatik* II. 1, p. 394.
[3] *Inst.* I. x. 2. C.R. II, p. 73.
[4] C.R. XXIII, p. 11. C.T.S. I, p. 64.

It remains to see of what religious value this revelation is to man. It does not, despite a sentence to the contrary in *Institutio I. vi.* 1, [1] lead us to salvation. That is to say, it does not bring to us the forgiveness of our sins and eternal life. We know God as Creator, not as Redeemer. We learn the very first lesson of religion—to be religious. And the nature of pure religion is this: "It consists in faith, joined with a serious fear of God, comprehending a voluntary reverence, and producing legitimate worship agreeable to the Law." [2] *Fides, timor, reverentia, cultus. Fides* here comprises both belief and trust; belief that God is, that He has revealed Himself to us in His works, and in His Word, that He is our Creator and Preserver, our loving Father, that there is no good thing that does not come from Him, and that nothing can occur upon the earth but what He wills. And trust that is assured that it may in all circumstances rely upon His help, that He will supply all needs and that under the shadow of His wing there is safety. "For at the very outset, the godly mind dreams not of some imaginary deity, but contemplates only the one true God; and indulges not in fictitious fancies about Him; but, content with believing Him to be such as He reveals Himself, uses the most diligent and unremitting caution lest it should fall into error by rash and presumptuous transgression of His will. He who thus knows Him, sensible that all things are subject to His control, trusts in Him as his Guardian and Protector, and unreservedly commits himself to His care. Assured that He the Author of all blessings, he immediately flies to His protection in distress or want, and awaits His aid. Persuaded of His goodness and mercy, he relies upon Him with unlimited trust, and does not doubt to find in His clemency a remedy provided for all his evils." [3]

Timor and *reverentia* are coupled in Calvin's mind, and the former is very little the stronger word. Only the ungodly should regard God with terror as a Judge. Believers should learn to fear Him as a son fears a loving father. The believer's fear of

[1] "Therefore not in vain has He added the light of His Word, to make Himself known unto salvation." C.R. II, p. 53. This strange statement must be set against the rest of I. vi. 1, especially from the words "I speak not yet of the peculiar doctrine of faith . . ." onwards, and they will be denuded of their force, and leave us wondering why ever Calvin used them.

[2] *Inst.* I. ii. 2. C.R. II, p. 35.

[3] Ibid.

God is a reverential love, a willing obedience and joyful submission to God. "Knowing Him to be his Lord and Father, he
concludes that he ought to mark His government in all things,
revere His majesty, endeavour to promote His glory, and obey
His commands. Perceiving Him to be a just Judge, armed with
severity for the punishment of crimes, he keeps His tribunal
always in mind, and is restrained by fear from provoking His
wrath. Yet, he is not so terrified at the apprehension of His
justice as to wish to evade it, even if escape were possible; but
loves Him as much in punishing the wicked as in blessing the
godly. . . . Besides, he restrains himself from sin, not merely
from a dread of vengeance, but because he loves and reveres God
as his Father, honours and worships Him as his Lord, and even
were there no hell, would shudder at the thought of offending
Him." [1]

The fruit of this faith, fear and reverence is worship. Without
it there cannot be said to be any knowledge of God, for "our
mind cannot conceive of God without ascribing some worship
to Him". [2] How much more, then, when we trust in God, fear
Him and love Him, should our hearts outflow towards Him in
worship. Yet such worship is rare. Many pay a formal worship
to God, but very few show by their heartfelt worship that pure
and genuine religion which springs from the first and simple
knowledge of God their Creator.

[1] *Inst.* I. ii. 2. C.R. II, p. 35.
[2] *Inst.* I. ii. 1. C.R. II, p. 34.

Theologia Gloriae aut Crucis?

"Now, in describing the world as a mirror in which we ought to behold God, I would not be understood to assert, either that our eyes are sufficiently clear-sighted to discern what the fabric of heaven and earth represents, or that the knowledge to be thus obtained is sufficient for salvation. And whereas the Lord invites us to Himself by the means of created things, with no other effect than that of thereby rendering us inexcusable, He has added, as was necessary, a new remedy, or at least, by a new aid He has assisted the ignorance of our mind. For by the Scripture as our guide and teacher (*Scriptura duce et magistra*), He not only makes those things plain which would otherwise escape our notice, but almost compels us to behold them—as if He had assisted our dull sight with spectacles. On this point, as we have already observed, Moses insists. For if the mute instruction of the heaven and earth were sufficient, the teaching of Moses would have been superfluous. This herald therefore approaches, who excites our attention to make us perceive that we are placed in this scene for the purpose of beholding the glory of God—not indeed, to perceive them as mere spectators, but to enjoy all the riches which are here exhibited, as the Lord has ordained and subjected them to our use. And he not only declares in general that God is the architect of the world, but through the whole chain of history he shows how wonderful is His power, His goodness, and, above all, His tender solicitude for the human race. Besides, since the eternal Word of God is His lively and express image, he recalls us to this point. And thus the assertion of the Apostle is verified, that through no other means than faith can it be understood, that the worlds were made by the Word of God (Heb, 11. 3). For faith properly proceeds from this, that, taught by the ministry of Moses, we do not now wander in foolish or trifling speculations, but contemplate the true and only God in His genuine image.

"It may, however, be objected that this seems at variance with what Paul declares: 'For after that in the wisdom of God the world by wisdom knew not God, it pleased God by the foolishness of preaching to save them that believe.' (I. Cor. 1. 21.) For

E

he thus intimates that God is sought in vain under the guidance of visible things; and that nothing remains for us but to betake ourselves immediately to Christ; and that we must not therefore commence with the elements of this world, but with the Gospel, which sets Christ only before us with His cross, and holds us to this one point. I answer, It is in vain for any to reason as philosophers on the workmanship of the world save those who, having been first humbled by the preaching of the Gospel, have learned to submit the whole of their intellectual wisdom (as Paul expresses it) to the foolishness of the cross (I Cor. 1. 21). I say that we shall find **nothing,** either above or below, which can raise us up to God, until Christ shall have instructed us in His own school. Yet, this cannot be done unless we, having emerged from out the lowest depths, are borne up above all heavens in the chariot of His cross, that there by faith we may apprehend those things which eye has never seen, nor ear heard, and which far surpass our hearts and minds. For the earth, with its supply of fruits for our daily nourishment, is not set before us there; but Christ offers Himself to us unto eternal life. Nor does heaven, by the shining of the sun and stars, enlighten our bodily eyes then, but the same Christ, the Light of the world and the Sun of righteousness, shines into our souls. Nor does the air stretch out there its empty space for us to breathe in, but the Spirit of God Himself quickens us and causes us to live. There, in short, the invisible kingdom of Christ fills all things, and His spiritual grace is diffused through all. Yet this does not prevent us from applying our senses to the consideration of heaven and earth, that we may thence seek confirmation in the true knowledge of God. For Christ is that image in which God presents to our view, not only His heart, but also His hands and His feet. I give the name of His *heart* to that secret love with which He embraces us in Christ: by His *hands* and *feet* I understand those works of His which are displayed before our eyes. As soon as ever we depart from Christ, there is nothing, be it never so gross and insignificant in itself, respecting which we cannot help being deceived." [1]

[1] *Argument to Commentary on Genesis.* C.R. XXIII, pp. 9–10. C.T.S. I, pp. 62–64.

Part Two
The Knowledge of the Redeemer

CHAPTER FOUR

THE DOCTRINE OF THE WORD OF GOD

1

THE WORD IN RELATION TO GOD

A NOT unusual comment on the *Institutio* has been that there was no change in its doctrine from the first edition to the last.[1] In many respects this is quite true, and chiefly in that the theological spirit that we associate with Calvin's name meets us in 1536 no less than in 1559. In other respects, however, it is only half-true, if that. This is so of his doctrine of the Trinity, which presents one of the most interesting of all the problems arising from his theology. The doctrine plays a small part only—though perfectly orthodox—in the first edition. In the subsequent editions, not only is more attention paid to it, but also it increasingly moulds the book into conformity with itself both in substance and in form. This latter is shown in the way that the Creed, with its four main articles, enters into the *Institutio* in 1543 and finally imposes its form upon the 1559 edition. We should pay little attention to the idea that, on the principle that where there is smoke there is also fire, Caroli had some good grounds for accusing Calvin of Arianism in 1537, and, at his instigation, Bucer and the Strasburg ministers for requiring him to sign an orthodox statement of belief, during his exile in that city. Even in the 1536 *Institutio*, his doctrine of the Trinity is perfectly orthodox.[2] The only basis for Caroli's accusation was the omission of the doctrine from the *Confession de la foy* of 1537, and the relatively small part it played in the 1536 *Institutio*. If we might hazard a conjecture (though based upon facts), we should say that when he wrote the first edition Calvin's knowledge of patristic theology was not extensive,[3] and

[1] *E.g.* "The work grew in compass in the successive editions, without any modification of its doctrines." G. P. Fisher: *History of Christian Doctrine* (Edinburgh, 1896), p. 298.

[2] It occurs in cap. II. *De Fide.* E.g. "*Scriptura unum nobis Deum tradit, non plures. Israel, inquit, Dominus Deus tuus Deus unus est (Deut. 6.). Eadem tamen et patrem Deum, et filium Deum, et spiritum sanctum Deum, nihil obscure asserit.*" C.R. I, p. 58.

[3] Here we must differ from Karl Holl who writes, with regard to assigning an early date to Calvin's conversion, as if he were already a great patristic scholar

was, moreover, somewhat swamped by the predominance of specifically reformed ideas (e.g: justification by faith alone) and by anti-Roman polemics (e.g. the chapter on the five "false" sacraments). Further study of the Fathers and Creeds, lasting throughout his life, showed him two things: that the Creeds were true expositions and arrangements of the teaching of the Scriptures; and that the orthodox doctrine of the Trinity said precisely what he himself wanted to say. The result is that in succeeding editions of the *Institutio* new quotations from the Fathers are being continually added; and the form of the book approximates to the Apostle's Creed until finally it becomes an exposition of it. The development of the *Institutio* does not portray an erring theologian's return to orthodoxy, but the enrichment of a true presentation of the Faith by the influx of ancient and traditional forms of orthodoxy.

When we speak of Calvin's doctrine of the Trinity or of his Christology as orthodox, however, we must beware lest we fail to do justice to him by making into merely academic concepts what for him were the very life-blood and power of his faith. Doumergue somewhere tells the story of the conversion of an Anabaptist by Calvin. And in what did this conversion consist? In the acknowledgment by the Anabaptist of the doctrine of the Trinity. This strikes strangely upon our modern ears, but beliefs that modern churches and Christians often consider proper to hold because they are part of the traditional theological furniture of the Church were for Calvin, as for the orthodox Fathers and School-men, the grounds of salvation, worth living for and dying for.

This attitude is apparent in the way in which he uses the doctrine of the pre-existence of Christ. It is no merely academic concept for him, but has become an integral part of his thinking. Hence, when he speaks of the Incarnation, he says as often as not, that "Christ appeared". "Our Lord then made His appearance as a real man"; [1] "*Quand nostre Seigneur Jesus est apparu au monde.*" [2] The Incarnation, he says, refuting Servetus,

by 1536: "He must have found time, alongside his legal studies, to acquire his imposing theological, and especially patristic, learning." (*Johannes Calvin* in *Gesämmelte Aufsätze* 3., p. 261). In fact, the 1536 *Institutio* is not remarkable for its dependence upon the past. Only 5 Fathers are directly cited: Ambrose (once), Augustine (ten times), Jerome, Sozomenus and Tertullian (once each).

[1] *Inst.* II. xii. 3. C.R. II, p. 341.
[2] *Sixth Sermon on Harmony of Gospels.* C.R. XLVI, p. 73.

did not mean "that Christ began to be the Son of God, which He was not before" but "that He was manifested among men in order that they might know Him to be the One who had been promised before". [1] The Incarnation was not the beginning of a new being, but a change in the form of the eternal Being: "He who had been the Son of God in His eternal Godhead, appeared also as the Son of God in human flesh". [2]

In his commentary on John 1. 1, Calvin makes a distinction between *Sermo* and *Verbum*. The Greek text runs: Ἐν ἀρχῇ ἦν ὁ Λόγος, καὶ ὁ Λόγος ἦν πρὸς τὸν Θεόν, καὶ Θεός ἦν ὁ Λόγος. For the translation of ὁ Λόγος "Latin theology wavered between *Verbum*, *Sermo* and *Ratio* before accepting *Verbum*, the least satisfactory, perhaps, of the three". [3] It was *Verbum* that was used in the Vulgate. But Erasmus went back to *Sermo* in his translation and Calvin followed him. *In principio erat Sermo.* In a brief note Calvin justifies the word: "I wonder at what induced the Latins to render ὁ Λόγος by *Verbum*, for that would have been the translation of τὸ ῥῆμα. But even allowing that they had some plausible reason, yet it cannot be denied that *Sermo* would have been far more appropriate. Hence it is evident how barbarous was the tyranny exercised by those theologasters who harassed Erasmus so greatly because he had changed one word for the better." [4]

It would appear that we have here the basis for a distinction universal in Calvin's writings and upon which a consistent doctrine can be built. In fact, we have nothing of the sort, for he uses the two words quite indiscriminately, even to the extent of using *Verbum* when he quotes John 1! [5] The most that can be said is that he always seems deliberately to couple together *aeternus* and *Sermo*, and never *aeternum* and *Verbum*, and that in general he uses *Sermo* rather than *Verbum* as the synonym of

[1] *In Luc.* 1. 32. C.R. XLV, p. 28. C.T.S. I, p. 37.
[2] *In Luc.* 1. 35. C.R. XLV, p. 31. C.T.S. I, p. 43.
[3] W. R. Inge: article *Logos* in *Hastings' Encyclopaedia of Religion and Ethics.* vol. 8, pp. 133-4.
[4] *In Joh.* 1. 1. C.R. XLVII, p. 3. C.T.S. I, p. 28.
[5] E. g. Luke 11. 28. has *Quinimo beati, qui audiunt sermonem Dei.* (C.R. XLV, p. 348.) This, when next quoted, becomes *Imo, inquit, beati qui audiunt verbum Dei.* (C.R. XLV, p. 348. ll. 34-35.) For John I. see *Inst.* I. xiii. 11. "And why should John, after having affirmed at the beginning of his Gospel, *verbum semper fuisse Deum. . . .*" (C.R. II, p. 99.) See also *Inst.* II. xiv. 1: *Porro quod dicitur, verbum carnem esse factum . . .*" C.R. II, p. 353.

sapientia Dei, though there are exceptions. Nevertheless, inconsistently as he may employ the terms, there is in this distinction the essence of his doctrine of the Word of God.

What do the Scriptures mean by *verbum Dei?* asks Calvin in *Institutio* I. xiii. 7–8. Certainly not simply *vox Dei*—the transient sound of God's voice spoken into the air, like the *oracula* and *prophetiae* which He spoke to the patriarchs; but rather "the eternal Wisdom residing in God whence proceeded all the oracles and prophecies". [1] Behind the word expressed is the word thought. Behind the *verbum Dei* is *Sapientia Dei*, or *aeternus Sermo Dei*. The Word was with God as His eternal Wisdom. This eternal Wisdom He expressed in the creation, when He created by His Word (which here means, "the nod or mandate of the Son, who is Himself *aeternus et essentialis Patris sermo*"). [2] As of the creation, so of every revelation of God. Revelation must be understood as the Word of God—that is, as the *verbum Dei* which is the temporal form of the *Sapientia Dei* ot *aeternus Sermo Dei*. "Therefore as all revelations proceeding from God do well bear the name of the word of God, so ought we yet to set in the highest place the substantial Word, the fountain of all oracles, which being subject to no alteration, abideth always one and the self-same with God, and is God Himself." [3]

Now let us turn to the Commentary on John 1. 1. There is in the Word of God, says Calvin, a *duplex relatio*. It relates on the one hand to God in that it is eternally *apud Deum;* and on the other hand to men, in that it is the revelation of God to men. In this consists the Scriptural meaning of the Word of God, "first, because He is the eternal Wisdom and Will of God; [4] and secondly, because He is the clear expression of His purpose (*expressa consilii eius effigies*); for, as speech is said among men to be the image of the mind, so it is not inappropriate to apply this to God, and to say that He expresses Himself to us by His Word spoken." [5] In His relation to God the Word is hidden and

---

[1]*Inst.* I. xiii. 7. C.R. II, p. 95.
[2]*Inst.* I. xiii. 7. C.R. II, p. 95.
[3]*Inst.* I. xiii. 7. C.R. II, p. 95.
[4]"If we are not at liberty to conceive of God without His Wisdom, it must be acknowledged that we ought not to seek the origin of the Word anywhere else than in the eternal Wisdom of God." *In Joh.* 1. 1. (C.R. XLVII, p. 2. C.T.S. I, p. 27.
[5]*In Joh.* 1. 1. C.R. XLVII, p. 1. C.T.S. I, p. 26.

incomprehensible: in His relation to men He is revealed and known. [1]

These two passages give us the essence of Calvin's doctrine of the Word of God, which, by the use of other passages also, we may now expand thus:

The necessity of the doctrine of the Trinity to Calvin's theology, which we stressed at the beginning of this chapter, becomes apparent. The essence of God is "simple and indivisible"; and He is the One beside whom there are and can be no equals. But in the one and indivisible God are, as orthodoxy had long taught, three Persons or Subsistences. Calvin is careful, however, to maintain that this is not merely an ecclesiastical dogma erected to defend the Faith against attacks from heretics, but is in substance, if not in terminology, Scriptural. [2] Thus the title of Book I, chapter xiii runs: "*Unicam Dei essentiam ab ipsa creatione tradi in scripturis. . . .*" [3] But if this doctrine comes from the Scriptures, it means that thus God reveals Himself. "He also designates Himself by another peculiar character, by which He may be yet more clearly distinguished; for while He declares Himself to be but One, He sets Himself forth to be distinctly considered in Three Persons, without apprehending which, we have only a bare and empty name of God floating in our minds, without any idea of the true God." [4] The Son, or the Word of God, or the Wisdom of God (for all these are names of the second Person of the Trinity), is a subsistence in the Divine essence, with a relation to the Father and the Holy Spirit, and yet distinguished from Them by an incommunicable property. The Son is of the same essence with the Father and the Spirit. If the essence of the Son were not the essence of God revelation would either not be revelation by the Word or it would not be the self-revelation of God. The *relatio* of the Son to the Father and the Spirit, or that which They have in common, is Godhead: "We particularly use the word *relatio* here, because, when mention is made simply and indefinitely of God,

---

[1] "The Word was, as it were, hidden before He revealed Himself in the external structure of the world."—*In Joh.* i. i. C.R. XLVII, p. 3. C.T.S. I, p. 27.
[2] See *Inst.* I. xiii. 3–5.
[3] C.R. II, p. 89.
[4] *Inst.* I. xiii. 2. C.R. II, p. 90.

this Name pertains no less to the Son and Spirit than to the Father".[1]

2

THE WORD AS REVELATION

As well as the relatedness, however, there exists a distinction between the Persons of the Godhead. Such a distinction as will preclude us from believing, with Praxeas, that the Father died upon the cross, or, with Lactantius, that ὁ λόγος and τὸ πνεῦμα are identical. The distinction of incommunicable properties consists in this: "that to the Father is attributed the principle of action, the fountain and source of all things; to the Son, wisdom, counsel, and the dispensation of all operations; and the power and efficacy of the action is assigned to the Spirit".[2] Yet, with the *distinctio* must be borne in mind at the same time the *relatio*. There can, since the essence of God is simple, be no question of one Person of the Trinity acting in isolation from the other Persons. Every work of God is the work of God Himself; that is, of the entire Godhead. Certainly the Son, and not the Father, died on the cross; but He died there in obedience to the will of the Father— "being delivered by the determinate counsel and foreknowledge of God".[3] Certainly the Word and the Spirit are not identical; but certainly also the Word and the Spirit work together and not apart from each other.

The property of the Word of God is, then, "wisdom, counsel, and the dispensation of all operations"—"*sapientia, consilium, et dispensatio in rebus agendis*". It is by His Word that God created and preserves the heavens and the earth and all life; it is by His Word that God redeems mankind; it is by His Word that God holds any communication with men. "*Sapientia, consilium, et dispensatio in rebus agendis*" means in effect that what God does towards us and in the world, He does by His Word; and in respect of revelation it means that "as all revelations proceeding from God do well bear the name of the Word of God, so ought we yet to set in the highest place the substantial Word, the fountain of

[1]*Inst*. I. xiii. 6. C.R. II, p. 94.
[2]*Inst*. I. xiii. 18. C.R. II, p. 104.
[3]Acts 2. 23.

all oracles, which, being subject to no alteration, abideth always one and the self-same with God, and is God Himself". [1]

Revelation is to be called the Word of God because it is the activity of God Himself working by His Word, or Son, or Wisdom. When the Word becomes revelation, it means that He assumes a form which is a contact with men within the sphere of their experience, and that this form reveals God Himself. It is when we come to consider these forms of revelation, that the doctrine of the Trinity is saved from becoming a product of speculation, and is seen to be the specific and unique knowledge of God that is the Christian faith. To be more precise, the doctrine of the Trinity is a *Christian* doctrine because of the Biblical declaration that the Son, Word, or Wisdom of God is to be identified with this particular man called Jesus of Nazareth. "Christ is the same Word clad with flesh," [2] says Calvin, echoing John I. 14. Here we need only observe that Calvin does so identify Jesus with the eternal Word, without following him through the proofs from Scripture that he gives in *Institutio* I. xiii. 9 ff. It is important to notice also, however, that they are proofs from Scripture. This identification is one which we can make in no other way than by faith, upon the basis of the Biblical witness to Jesus Christ. When we think of the Word of God, therefore, we are not to imagine to ourselves an unknown and mysterious Being; we are to think of Jesus of Nazareth.

Calvin applies the principle "by Christ alone" not only to his own time and to the exclusion of salvation by works, but to all ages. "Since the Fall of the first man, no knowledge of God has been available for salvation apart from the Mediator." [3] It was Christ who appeared as the Angel of God, and "who even then began to perform some services introductory to His execution of the office of Mediator. For though He was not yet incarnate, He descended in a mediatorial capacity, as it were, that He might approach the faithful with greater familiarity". [4] It was Christ who, according to St. Paul led "the people in the wilderness; because, though the time of His humiliation was not yet arrived, the eternal Word then exhibited a type of the office to which He

---

[1] *Inst.* I. xiii. 7. C.R. II, p. 95.
[2] *Inst.* I. xiii. 9. C.R. II, p. 96.
[3] *Inst.* II. vi. I. C.R. II, p. 248.
[4] *Inst.* I. xiii. 10. C.R. II, p. 98.

was appointed".[1] He it was who in the Old Testament was promised as the Redeemer, and put before the Patriarchs as the object of their faith;[2] and, in fact, "from the beginning of the world He has always been manifested to all the elect, that they might look to Him, and place all their trust in Him".[3] Hence, as it was in His Word alone (i.e. in the oracles of God and in the O.T.) that the Mediator was manifested, "all mankind, except the Jews, as they sought God without the Word, must necessarily have been wandering in vanity and error".[4]

The Law (that is, not only the Decalogue, "but the form of religion delivered from God by the hands of Moses"[5]—in other words, the heart of the Old Testament) witnesses to Christ. It was given "not to draw away the attention of the chosen people from Christ, but rather to keep their minds waiting for His advent, to inflame their desires and confirm their expectations".[6] The Commandments witness to Him in an indirect manner by convicting of sin. By the Law we learn to know ourselves as sinners, and this self-knowledge is "the true and only preparation for seeking Christ".[7] This was so no less for the Jews before the Incarnation than for all men since. It was in Christ that they believed and by His atonement that they were forgiven. The legal ceremonies had no efficacy of their own to make atonement, but bore witness to Christ. "From the Law, therefore, we may properly learn Christ, if we consider that the covenant which God made with the Fathers was founded on the Mediator; that the sanctuary, by which God manifested the presence of His grace, was consecrated by His blood; that the Law itself, with its promises, was sanctioned by the shedding of blood; that a single priest was chosen out of the whole people, to appear in the presence of God in the name of all, not as an ordinary mortal, but clothed in sacred garments; and that no hope of reconciliation with God was held out to men but through the offering of sacrifice."[8]

[1]*Inst.* I. xiii. 10. C.R. II, p. 98.
[2]*Inst.* II. vi. 2. C.R. II, pp. 248–250.
[3]*Inst.* II. vi. 4. C.R. II, p. 252.
[4]*Inst.* I. vi. 4. C.R. II, p. 56.
[5]*Inst.* II. vii. 1. C.R. II, pp. 252–3.
[6]*Inst.* II. vii. 1. C.R. II, p. 252.
[7]*Inst.* II. vii. 2. C.R. II, p. 254.
[8]*In Luc.* 24. 27. C.R. XLV, p. 807. C.T.S. III, p. 361

Before His Incarnation, however, Christ revealed Himself comparatively indistinctly. "For it was reasonable that before the Sun of righteousness was risen, there should be neither such a full blaze of revelation, nor such great clearness of understanding. Therefore the Lord dispensed the Light of His Word to them in such a manner, that they had yet only a distant and obscure prospect of it." [1] But the revelation increased in clarity; God made Himself known more and more clearly to His people. "For this is the order and economy which God observed in dispensing the covenant of His mercy, that as the course of time accelerated the period of its full exhibition, He clarified it from day to day with additional revelations. Thus, in the beginning, when the first promise was given to Adam, it was like the kindling of some feeble sparks. Subsequent accessions caused a considerable magnifying of the light, which continued to increase more and more, and diffused its splendour over a wide extent, until at length, every cloud being dispersed, Christ, the Sun of righteousness, completely illuminated the whole world." [2] The revelation was not the less real for being dim, for it was God who revealed Himself. But all this, says Calvin, obscurely until the advent of Jesus Christ.

[1] *Inst.* II. xi. 5. C.R. II, p. 333.
[2] *Inst.* II. x. 20. C.R. II, p. 326.

CHAPTER FIVE

THE REVELATION OF THE SON OF GOD

1

JESUS AND REVELATION

The identification of Jesus of Nazareth with the eternal Word of God, made by faith on the authority of the Scriptural witness, means that He is regarded as the valid revelation of God. On the one hand, as the eternal Word He is God, and therefore His appearing is the revelation of God Himself. If He were not God the representation would be false; we should see in Him the image of something, but not of God. Since, however, He is that eternal Word, He presents to us the *imago patris*. On the other hand, His humanity, the form of the revelation, provides the proximity of God to man without which man, unable to rise above his humanity, cannot know God. In Jesus God comes near to men.

But the Word did not become flesh merely for purposes of intelligibility. To say this would be to misunderstand the position between men and God; as if they had only to have God presented to them in an intelligible manner to know Him. Whereas in fact the knowledge of God constitutes a moral as well as an intellectual problem. The revelation of Jesus Christ is the revelation of the forgiveness of sins by God through Jesus Christ. It is revelation that is in itself redemption. "Paul means not only that Christ is the pledge of all the blessings that God has ever promised, but that we have in Him a full and complete exhibition of them . . . And indeed, the freely bestowed adoption, by which we are made sons of God, as it proceeds from the good pleasure which the Father had from eternity, has been revealed to us in this respect, that Christ (who alone is the Son of God by nature) has clothed Himself with our flesh and made us His brethren." [1]

Calvin treats these two ideas—of the nearness of God in

---

[1] *Argument to Comm. on Harmony of Gospels.* C.R. XLV, p. i. C.T.S. I, p. xxxvi.

Christ, and of revelation as redemption—together. It was necessary for Christ to humble His state to manhood because man was unable to exalt himself to fellowship with God. And that, not only beçause God is transcendent and inaccessible ("Although man had remained immaculately innocent, his condition would have been too mean for him to approach to God without a Mediator"), [1] but far more because our sins remove us from God's gracious presence and hide Him from us. Unless, then, Christ should come to us, and as God and man be a Mediator to reconcile us to God, we should have no hope. *Emmanuel*, God with us, means the redemptive proximity of God. God hath visited—and redeemed His people. "Scripture commonly says that God is with us when He is present with us in His help and grace, and puts forth the power of His arm to protect us. But here is expressed the way in which God communicates with men, for outside Christ we are alienated from Him; but by Christ we are not only received into His grace, but are made one with Him." [2] Elsewhere he calls Christ "*speculum inaestimabilis Dei gratiae*". [3]

The Incarnation of the Son of God is thus a necessity; but not a simple or absolute necessity. [4] That is to say, it was not a necessity arising from either the nature of God or of man, but from the nature of the case (using that word both in its precise meaning and also generally!). It was necessary for the creation and fallen man that Christ should become man, so that on Him might be built the new creation and in Him might be created the new man. Would Christ have become man if man had not sinned? This question, agitated by Osiander, Calvin will not answer in a final manner, though he censures Osiander's treatment of the matter. Instead, he adheres to his principle of *Scriptura sola*, and says that, according to the Scriptures, the Incarnation and Redemption are always united. To investigate the matter further is to throw aside obedience to the Scriptures and the Holy Spirit who teaches us there: "since the whole Bible proclaims that He was clothed in flesh in order to become a Redeemer, it argues excessive temerity to imagine another cause

[1] *Inst.* II. xii. 1. C.R. II, p. 340.
[2] *In Matt.* 1. 23. C.R. XLV, p. 68. C.T.S. I, p. 105.
[3] *Inst.* II. xiv. 5. C.R. II, pp. 356-7.
[4] *Inst.* II. xii. 1. C.R. II, p. 340.

or another end for it. The end for which Christ was promised
from the beginning is sufficiently known: it was to restore a
fallen world and to succour ruined men". [1]

When we speak of Jesus Christ, however, we must be sure that
we have in mind the true Christ. For it is easily possible to
conceive of Him a false image which does not correspond with
the Scriptural witness to Him. We are all too apt, says Calvin,
"to love something other than Christ under the name of Christ." [2]
This was the great heresy of the Papacy, that in its theology
Christ was "obscured". "This evil then, as well as innumerable
others, must be imputed to the schoolmen, who have, as it were,
concealed Christ." [3]   Roman Christology was orthodox and
traditional, but it was no more than that. Christ was not put in
the supreme position of unique Redeemer, says Calvin. "The
reason why the Papists have nothing more than a shadow of
Christ, is that they have been careful to look at His mere essence,
but have disregarded His kingdom, which consists in the power
to save." [4] It is for this reason that he repudiates worship of the
Blessed Virgin, since it detracts from the glory of Christ: "For
Mary has been constituted the Queen of Heaven, the Hope, the
Life, and the Salvation of the world; and, in short, their fury and
madness proceeded so far that they stripped Christ of His spoils,
and left Him almost naked". [5]

The most important work that the Reformation accomplished
was to restore the true Christ to His rightful place. Time after
time after time we find Luther and Calvin, Melanchthon,
Zwingli and Bucer, Cranmer and Ridley and Jewel, and all the
other major and minor reformers declaring, emphasizing and
explaining, in sermons and in books, at their supper tables and
at public disputations this major article of faith: Christ alone.
The true meaning of the Reformation is that it was a widespread
and intensive witness to Jesus Christ. Luther perceived very
clearly the absolute centrality of this doctrine, and wrote: "I
have learned and noticed in all the histories of Christianity, that
those who have held and kept to the chief article of Jesus Christ

---

[1] *Inst.* II. xii. 4. C.R. II, p. 342.
[2] *In Joann.* 14. 21. C.R. XLVII, p. 331. C.T.S. II, p. 96.
[3] *Inst.* III. ii. 2. C.R. II, p. 398.
[4] *In Joann.* 1. 49. C.R. XLVII, p. 36. C.T.S. I, p. 79.
[5] *In Joann.* 2. 4. C.R. XLVII, p. 39. C.T.S. I, pp. 84-5.

have remained safe and sure in the true Christian faith. And although they have erred and sinned in other respects, yet they have been preserved in the end. He who holds to the doctrine that Jesus Christ is true God and true man, who died and rose again for us, will acquiesce in and heartily assent to all the other articles of the Christian faith . . . on the other hand, I have also observed that all errors, heresies, idolatries, offences, abuses and ungodliness in the Church have arisen primarily because this article, or part, of the Christian faith concerning Jesus Christ has been either disregarded or abandoned. Clearly and rightly viewed, it is plain that all heresies militate against this precious article concerning Jesus Christ". [1]

Calvin stands firmly within the true Reformation position, which is indeed to say, within the true Christian position, for what is Christianity if it is not indissolubly bound up with Jesus Christ? Apart from Christ we have no knowledge of God, he says; no salvation and no blessing from God. Apart from Him we wander in a maze; if seeking God, ever seeking, never finding. Who is God? He is the Father of Jesus Christ, in whom, the true *imago patris*, He has revealed Himself. "Now this is a remarkable sentence, and ought to be reckoned among the first axioms of our religion: yea, when we have confessed that there is one true God, this second article ought necessarily to be added, that He is no other but He who is made known in Christ. The Apostle does not here treat distinctly of the unity of essence. It is, indeed, certain that the Son cannot be disunited from the Father, for He is of the same essence ($\delta\mu oo\acute{u}\sigma\iota os$); but something other is spoken of here; that is, that the Father, who is invisible, has revealed Himself only in His Son. Hence He is called the image of the Father (Heb. 1. 3) because He sets forth and exhibits to us all that is necessary to be known of the Father. For the naked majesty of God would, by its immense brightness, ever dazzle our eyes; it is therefore necessary for us to look upon Christ. . . . John calls us to this practical part of faith, that as God has given Himself to us to be enjoyed only in Christ, He is elsewhere sought for in vain; or, if anyone prefers to have it still clearer, that since all the fullness of the Deity dwells in Christ, there is no

---

[1] *Die drei Symbola, oder Bekenntnis des Glaubens Christi, in der Kirche einträchtiglich gebraucht.* 1538. *Erlangen Ausgabe* 23, pp. 258-9.

F

God apart from Him." [1]   By this final Luther-like blast he certainly does not intend to deny the Father and the Spirit, but means that we cannot conceive of God even, far less know Him as a Father, apart from Christ. *"To know Thee and Jesus Christ whom Thou hast sent.* The reason why he says this is, because there is no other way in which God is known but in the face of Jesus Christ, who is the bright and lively image of Him." [2] And again, on the same chapter: *"But I have known Thee, and these have known that Thou hast sent me.* Christ does not merely say that God was known by the disciples, but mentions two steps: first, that He has known the Father; and secondly, that the disciples have known that He was sent by the Father. But, as He adds immediately afterwards that He has declared to them the name of the Father, He praises them, as I have said, for the knowledge of God which separates them from the rest of the world. Yet we must attend to the order of faith, as it is here described. The Son came forth from the bosom of the Father, and properly speaking, He alone knows the Father; and therefore all who desire to approach God must betake themselves to Christ meeting them, and must devote themselves to Him; and after having been known by the disciples He will, at length, raise them to God the Father". [3]

Jesus of Nazareth is the revelation of God. What does this mean? That in Him God, formerly either hidden, or if known, known only obscurely, and even then by a revelation dependent upon this revelation, has shown Himself. "What had been hidden in God is revealed to us in Christ as man; and life, which was

---

[1] *In I Joann.* 2. 22. C.R. LV, p. 325. C.T.S., p. 196. Cf., for an example of Luther's insistence on this same idea, the passage in his commentary on Galatians, called *A rule to be observed, that men ought to abstaine from the curious searching of God's Majestie.* (W. A. 40 : 1, pp. 75 ff. Eng. Trans. 1635, pp. 16 ff.) Thus: "Whensoever thou hast to doe therefore in the matter of justification, and disputeth with thy selfe how God is to be found that justifieth and accepteth sinners: where and in what sort he is to be sought: then know thou that there is no other God besides this man Christ Jesus. Embrace him and cleave to him with thy whole heart, setting aside all curious speculations of the divine Majesty: For that he that is a searcher of God's Majesty shall be overwhelmed of his glory." (W.A. 40 : 1, p. 78. E. T. p. 17a.)
[2] *In Joann.* 17. 3. C.R. XLVII, p. 376. C.T.S. II, p. 166. Cf. C. F. Andrews' striking and beautiful description of his early Christian life: "it was Christ now who was in all my thoughts, and His face was ever before me when I thought of God." (*What I Owe to Christ.* London. 1933, p. 43.)
[3] *In Joann.* 17. 25. C.R. XLVII, p. 390. C.T.S. II, p. 188.

formerly inaccessible, is now placed before our eyes." [1] He is the "visible representation" or the "lively image" of the invisible God: "the Son is said to know the Father, not because He reveals Him by His Spirit, but because, being the lively image of Him, He represents Him visibly in His own person". [2] We have already discussed the concept of *image*, in regard to the revelation in the Creation. "The universe," we said, "is a mirror in which is to be seen the *effigies Dei*, the portrait of God. As such it is the image of God." [3] Calvin uses the same terminology of Jesus Christ, for it is a fundamental idea in his doctrine of revelation. He, the Word made flesh, is a mirror reflecting the *effigies Dei*, and hence He is the image of God. But although the same terminology is used, a different significance is given to it. The universe is the *speculum Dei* because it is His creation, and so bears the unmistakable marks of His workmanship. It is the *imago Dei* because it is the *speculum Dei*—and not conversely. That is to say, the fact that it is the mirror of God confers upon it the title of being the image of God. With Jesus, however, the precise opposite is true. He is the *speculum Dei* because He is, in Himself, as the eternal Word made flesh, the *imago Dei*. He reflects the *effigies Dei* because He is Himself God. "*Who is the image of the invisible God*. He mounts yet higher in discoursing of the glory of Christ. He calls Him the image of the invisible God, meaning by this that it is in Him alone that God, who is otherwise invisible, is manifested to us . . . I am well aware in what sense the Fathers were accustomed to explain this; for, having a contest to maintain against the Arians, they insist upon the equality of the Son with the Father, and His ὁμοουσίαν— identity of essence, while in the meantime they make no mention of what is the chief point: in what manner the Father makes Himself known in Christ. . . . In order, then, that we may not receive anything but what is solid, let us take notice, that the term image is not made use of in respect to essence, but with reference to us. For Christ is called the image of God on this ground, that He makes God, in a manner, visible to us. At the same time we also gather from this His ὁμοουσία, for Christ would not truly represent God if He were not the essential Word

[1] *In Joann.* 5. 27. C.R. XLVII, p. 119. C.T.S. I, p. 208.
[2] *In Matt.* 11. 27. C.R. XLV, p. 320. C.T.S. II, pp. 41–2.
[3] See p. 18.

of God, inasmuch as the question here is not about those things which by communication are suitable also to creatures, but the question is as to the perfect wisdom, goodness, righteousness and power of God, for the representing of which no creature is competent. . . . The sum is this, that God in Himself, that is, in His naked majesty, is invisible, and that, not to the eyes of the body merely, but also to men's understandings, and that He is revealed to us in Christ alone, that we may behold Him as in a mirror. For in Christ He shows us His righteousness, goodness, wisdom, power—in short, His entire self. We must beware of seeking Him elsewhere, for everything that would set itself up as a representation of God, apart from Christ, will be an idol." [1]

That the knowledge of God is by revelation and hence under a form, means that it is indirect. Since to see Him in His essence would destroy us, it is necessary that if He show Himself to us, He shall do so under a form that shall be within our experience, and shall neither harm us nor drive us away from Him, but shall—as Calvin was fond of saying in his sermons—"gently allure us to Him". Thus the revelation or unveiling of God is always at the same time His self-veiling. The forms under which He reveals Himself, as Luther stressed, are covering forms. [2] The Incarnation of the Son of God was such a veiled revelation. In Him was revealed the fullness of Divinity, but revealed under a form that concealed it: "the glory of Christ's Divinity . . . appeared under a veil of infirmity". [3] The hiddenness of the revelation in Jesus Christ consists in the fact that God is not man and is different from man, and for God to become man is for Him to assume a form that because it is foreign to Him, conceals Him. Kierkegaard has said that the fact that Christ was a lowly man was not the heart of the paradox, God-man; if He had been a prince the paradox and miracle would still

[1] *In Col.* 1. 15. C.R. LII, pp. 84-5. C.T.S., pp. 149-150.

[2] "It is therefore madness to enter into much disputation concerning God, as to what He was beyond and before time: for that is to desire to comprehend naked divinity, or the naked divine essence. And it is for this very reason that God has enwrapped Himself in the veils of His works, and under certain visible appearances: just as at this day He veils Himself under baptism, etc. If you depart from these veiling signs, you at once run away, beyond measure, beyond place, and beyond time, into the most absolute nothing, concerning which, as philosophers justly say, there can be no knowledge."—*in Gen.* 1. 2. *Weimar Ausgabe* XLII, p. 10.

[3] *In Matt.* 12. 17. C.R. XLV, p. 330. C.T.S. II, p. 58.

have been present. This is, of course, true; yet that Jesus was a lowly man instead of a prince was no work of supererogation, for to believe that a lowly-born, lowly-living and wretchedly executed man is God, although it adds nothing to the primary miracle that God should become man, does make the Deity of Christ more hidden before men, who have the preconceived conception of God as always powerful, majestic, successful, etc. The revelation in Jesus was veiled, therefore, not only in that He was man, but that He was *such* a man—that He was born in a stable, lived in a poor home, was frequently homeless, was the associate of poor and outcast people, and died, Himself an outcast, under the legal curse of God. "Christ's humility consisted in His abasing Himself from the highest pinnacle of glory to the lowest ignominy." [1]

Dr. Brunner warns us against discussing "how it is possible that God should become man". [2] Calvin also leaves this question alone, and is content with stating what the Incarnation meant to Christ and to us. He rejects decisively the idea of *kenosis* in favour of *krypsis*. When Christ became man, His Godhead was in no way diminished. He remained that self-same Word who was eternally with God: "For the Son of God miraculously descended from heaven; yet in such a manner that He never left heaven; He chose to be miraculously conceived in the Virgin's womb, to live on earth, and to hang on the cross; and yet He never ceased to fill the universe in the same manner as from the beginning". [3] Calvin interprets *emptying* in Philippians 2. 7 as being simply the self-abasement of Christ: "This emptying is the same as the abasement, as to which we shall see later. The expression, however, is used for the sake of emphasis to mean 'being brought to nothing'. Christ, indeed, could not divest Himself of Godhead; but He kept it concealed for a time, that it might not be seen, under the weakness of the flesh. Hence He laid aside His glory from the sight of men, not by lessening it, but by concealing it." [4]

[1]*In Phil.* 2. 6. C.R. LII, p. 25. C.T.S., p. 54.
[2]*The Mediator*. (Eng. Trans. by Olive Wyon. London, 1934), p. 322 n.
[3]*Inst*. II. xiii. 4. C.R. II, p. 352.
[4]*In Phil.* 2. 7. C.R. LII, p. 26. C.T.S., pp. 56–7. Cf. *Inst.* II. xiii. 2. "he did put on the image of a servant, and contented with that humility, suffered his Godhead to be hidden with the veil of his flesh." And "for a time the glory of his Godhead did not shine forth, but only the shape of a man (*humana species*) appeared in base and abject state." (C.R. II, p. 349.)

There are two ways in which, following Calvin, we may relate
the two sides of this paradox, revelation-concealment. The one
is to see the very abasement, which is concealment, as revelation
of God. This we shall consider in the next section as Revelation
and Redemption. The other, which relates rather to our present
line of enquiry, is to think of the revelation in Christ as His
occasionally making Himself known, or stepping forth, as it
were, from behind the veil of concealment. This He did in two
ways, by His words and His works (thus acting, as God incarnate,
in the way in which He had worked from the beginning).

Although Jesus was in Himself the Son of God, He did not
reveal Himself until His baptism, but "remained in concealment,
during thirty years, as a private individual, because the time for
His manifestation was not yet come. But when He intended to
make Himself known to the world, He began with His baptism". [1]
The episode, related in Luke 2, of His questioning the doctors in
the Temple, was "a sort of prelude to His public calling". [2]
When, however, He had been baptized, He began to reveal Himself as the Son of God by preaching and by miracles.

The preaching of Jesus occupies a special and clearly defined
position in Calvin's Christology. He came "to be a preacher
and witness of the grace of the Father". [3] But His preaching was
different from all other preaching in this, that whereas other
preachers must point away from themselves to Christ, He draws
the attention of all men to Himself. For Calvin, Jesus is certainly
the prophet and the teacher, but He is not the teacher of liberal
Christianity, whose task, according to T. R. Glover, was "to
induce men to rethink God. Men, he saw, do not want precepts;
they do not want ethics, morals or rules; what they do need is to
rethink God, to re-discover Him, to re-explore Him, to live on
the basis of relation with God". [4] He did not point men away
from Himself to a God that He could tell them about, but drew
them to Himself as their God come to them in mercy and love.
"He proves from the effect that we ought not to seek God anywhere else than in Himself; for He maintains that His teaching,
being heavenly and truly divine, is a proof and bright mirror of

[1] *In Joann.* 1. 32. C.R. XLVII, p. 28. C.T.S. I, p. 68.
[2] *In Luc.* 2. 46. C.R. XLV, p. 105. C.T.S. I, p. 169.
[3] *Inst.* II. xv. 2. C.R. II, p. 362.
[4] *The Jesus of History.* (London, 1919), p. 72.

the presence of God. If it be objected, that all the Prophets ought
to be accounted sons of God because they speak divinely from
the inspiration of the Spirit and because God was the author of
their teaching, the answer is easy. We ought to consider the
substance of their teaching; for the Prophets send their disciples
to another person, but Christ attaches them to Himself." [1]

Moreover, the *doctrina Christi* was not a bare schoolroom
lesson, but contained the power of His Holy Spirit; such power
as to convince men of its truth, such authority as to amaze its
hearers, who perceived gladly or grudgingly that they were listen-
ing to something unusual. The power of the Holy Spirit and
the authority of God were in His preaching, and they miraculously declared Him to be the Son of God. "*I do not speak
from myself;* that is, as a man only, or after the manner of men;
because the Father, exhibiting the power of His Spirit in Christ's
teaching, wishes His Divinity to be recognized in Him. *The
Father Himself doeth the works.* This must not be confined to
miracles, for it is rather a continuation of the former statement,
that the majesty of God is clearly exhibited in Christ's teaching;
as if He had said, that His teaching is truly a work of God, from
which it may be known with certainty that God dwelleth in
Him." [2]

His miracles also, working together with His teaching, are
proofs of His identity, revelations of His Deity: "He was not
known as the Son of God by the external form of His body, but
because He gave illustrious proofs of His divine power, so that
the majesty of the Father shone forth in Him, as in a living and
distinct image". [3] This was true of all the miracles in general:
"We know that Christ did not perform miracles for the sake of
amusement, but had a definite object in view, which was to
prove that He was the Son of God and the appointed Redeemer
of the world". [4] And Calvin also usually points it out when
commenting upon particular miracles. Thus, on the raising of
Lazarus, he says: "Christ gave a remarkable proof of His divine
power in raising Lazarus". [5] Or when he calls the first miracle

[1] *In Joann.* 14. 10. C.R. XLVII, p. 326. C.T.S. II, pp. 87–8.
[2] *In Joann.* 14. 10. C.R. XLVII. p. 326. C.T.S. II, p. 88.
[3] *In I Joann.* 1. 1. C.R. LV, p. 300. C.T.S., p. 159.
[4] *In Matt.* 12. 16. C.R. XLV, p. 330. C.T.S. II, p. 57.
[5] *In Joann.* 11. 1. C.R. XLVII, p. 255. C.T.S. I, p. 424.

that He wrought, in Cana of Galilee, "the first proof of His divinity". [1]

A similar difficulty arises with the miracles as with Christ's teaching. They were not unambiguous proofs of His Deity, because others, who were not God, and did not claim to be God, had worked miracles. But, says Calvin, although it is commonly objected, that He did not perform more or greater miracles than Moses and the Prophets "the answer is well known, that Christ is more eminent in miracles in this respect, that He was not merely a minister like the rest, but was properly the Author of them; for He employed His own name, His own authority and His own power in performing miracles". [2] What, however, of miracles performed by false prophets and evil spirits? How do we know whether Christ casts out devils by Beelzebub the prince of the devils, or by the finger of God? Only by faith, says Calvin. Many either failed to understand or else deliberately misunderstood Christ's miracles; the one saying "of a truth a prophet is come into the world," and the other "he casteth out devils by Beelzebub". But those who by His works believed in Christ, did so simply by faith, accepting the true meaning of the miracles and rejecting the false. "To whatever extent Satan may, like an ape, counterfeit the works of God in the dark, yet when the eyes are opened and the light of spiritual wisdom shines, miracles are a sufficiently powerful attestation of the presence of God." [3]

The principal miracle was the Resurrection. By it Jesus shows clearly that he is the Lord over death. He comes from above into humanity's world, even into humanity's death, and rises again by His divine power out of that death into His eternal glory. During His life in the flesh His Deity, though present, was hidden. His witness to Himself was, as it were, an exhortation to believe in spite of appearances, and His miracles were so many bright flashes of lightning in the darkness of the night. His Resurrection, however, was the clear light of the day, the manifestation of His divine and eternal glory as the *aeternus Sermo Dei*. "The mean and despicable condition of Christ which they saw with their eyes, while, clothed with the flesh, He was not at all

[1] *In Joann.* 2. 11. C.R. XLVII, p. 41. C.T.S. I, p. 89.
[2] *In Joann.* 15. 24. C.R. XLVII, pp. 352–3. C.T.S. II, pp. 128–9.
[3] *In Joann.* 3. 2. C.R. XLVII, p. 53. C.T.S. I, p. 107.

different from other men, prevented them from submitting to
His divine power. But now by, as it were, drawing back the veil,
He calls them to behold His heavenly glory, as if He had said,
'Because without honour I converse among men, I am despised
by you, and you recognise in Me nothing that is divine; but
before long God will adorn Me with splendid power, and with-
drawing Me from the contemptible state of mortal life, will raise
me above the heavens.' For in the resurrection of Christ, so
great was the power displayed by the Holy Spirit, that it plainly
showed Him to be the Son of God, as Paul also shows (Rom. 1:4.)
And when it is said, Thou art my Son, this day have I begotten
Thee (Ps. 2 : 7) the resurrection is brought forward as a proof
from which the glory of Christ ought to be acknowledged, and
His ascension to heaven was the completion of that Glory."[1]

2

THE REVELATION OF REDEMPTION

We must repeat that the work of Christ did not lie simply in
showing the Father to men able, and perhaps even willing, to
behold Him. The liberal interpretation of the revealing office of
Christ as merely showing men the character of God obscures
His central mission as the one who made reconciliation between
God and men. He does not show God to men capable of the
visio Dei, but opens their eyes that they may see Him. He is not
a mutual acquaintance bringing into renewed fellowship two
friends who have lost touch with each other, but a Mediator of
the grace of God to rebellious sinners, destroying that rebellion,
and as a good Mediator leading them back to God and reconciling them to Him. We cannot consider the revelation of God in
Christ apart from, or, indeed, in any way as different from, the
reconciliation of God in Christ. It is true that Calvin speaks of
Jesus revealing the Father in His teaching—"God was made
known to the world by the teaching of Christ".[2] But this is to be
understood as teaching about God's attitude towards us in

---

[1] *In Joann.* 6. 62. C.R. XLVII, pp. 158–9. C.T.S. I, pp. 272–3.
[2] *In Joann.* 17. 4. C.R. XLVII, pp. 377–8. C.T.S. II, p. 168.

Christ, not about God *in abstracto*.   Jesus revealed in His preaching the gracious mercy of God shown in Himself; He preached the Gospel of forgiveness and redemption.   Hence, His preaching was a part of His redemptive activity—as necessary a part as His "offices" of priest and king.

Jesus is the revelation of the grace of God.   Frequently in the Commentaries on the four Gospels, Calvin speaks of Christ as "exhibiting" the grace, etc. of God.   "Paul means, not only that Christ is the pledge of all the blessings that God has ever promised, but that we have in Him a full and complete exhibition of them." [1]   Or: "the treasures of the grace of God would be exhibited to the world in Christ". [2]   Or again: "True, indeed, the fountain of life, righteousness, virtue and wisdom is with God, but to us it is a hidden and inaccessible fountain.   But an abundance of those things is exhibited to us in Christ, that thence we may be permitted to seek them". [3]   Here again, however, this *exhibitio gratiae Dei* must not be construed to mean a simple showing forth of God's goodwill to men.   The substance and the manner of the exhibition are one, in that it is a redemptive exhibition, an exhibition of the *grace* of God; and that means, of the forgiveness of God in the incarnate, crucified and risen Christ.   This exhibition is effected by teaching the grace of God, by showing with miracles actually and typically that God is gracious, and—simply by the fact of His incarnation, life, death and resurrection.   In other words, *exhibitio gratiae Dei* means that Jesus Himself in, and not in spite of, His humiliation, is the revelation of the grace of God.   Whereas in the first part of this chapter we considered the humiliation of Christ as the voluntary concealment of His glory, through which, as the sun through clouds, He "shone forth" when He willed, by word and work until in His resurrection He stood plainly revealed in His glory, we have now to consider the Incarnation and all that it implies of humiliation as in itself the revelation of God.   This is the principal idea of the Christological section of the *Institutio*— Book II.   For this reason Calvin begins the Book with an uncompromising insistence upon the sin of all men and the ability of no man to know God.   Also, when he comes to discuss the

[1] *Arg. Comm. on Harm. Gosp.* C.R. XLV, p. 1. C.T.S. I, p. xxxvi.
[2] *In Matt.* 11. 4. C.R. XLV, p. 300. C.T.S. II, p. 9.
[3] *In Joann.* 1. 16. C.R. XLVII, p. 16. C.T.S. I, p. 50.

question *Cur Deus homo?* in chapter 12, he places the necessity in man's sin and God's mercy. The work of the Mediator was to reveal the redemption of God.

In the statement that Jesus reveals the grace of God by His humiliation and suffering, there are expressed the two cardinal ideas in Calvin's doctrine of the Incarnation: the work of Christ is the work of God; and Christ's work is voluntary.

Athanasius poses, in his customary clear-eyed way, the dilemma with which, as it were, God was confronted when man sinned. "It would, of course, have been unthinkable that God should go back upon His word and that man, having transgressed, should not die; but it was equally monstrous that beings which once had shared the nature of the Word should perish and turn back again into non-existence through corruption. . . . As, then, the creatures whom He had created reasonable, like the Word, were in fact perishing, and such noble works were on the road to ruin, what then was God, being Good, to do?" [1] The same question underlies the first four sections of *Institutio* II. xvi., though there it is asked in the form of how God could love us and hate us [2] until "He was reconciled to us in Christ". The consequence of the Fall was not purely subjective, but primarily it placed man in a new relationship with God. Whereas before, God had been the Creator-Father, blessing man with all good things, He now became also the Avenger, cursing man and his world on account of sin. "What then was God, being Good, to do?"

The answer stands in the Incarnation of the Son of God; and only when both sides of this dilemma become inescapable for us do we understand the significance of Jesus Christ. "For God, who is the highest righteousness, cannot love wickedness which he seeth in us all. Therefore we all have in us that which deserves God's hatred. Therefore in respect of our corrupted nature, and then of evil life added unto it, truly we all are subject to God's displeasure, guilty in his sight, and born to damnation of hell. But because the Lord will not lose that which is his in us, he findeth yet somewhat that he of his goodness may love. For

---

[1] *De Incarnatione* § 6. (Eng. Trans. by A Religious of C.S.M.V. London, 1944.)
[2] Thus Calvin quotes Augustine: "in a wonderful and divine manner he both hated and loved us at the same time". (*Inst.* II. xvi. 4. C.R. II, p. 370.)

howsoever we be sinners by our own fault, yet we remain his creatures. Howsoever we have purchased death to ourselves, yet he made us unto life. So is he moved by mere and free loving of us to receive us into favour. But since there is a perpetual and unappeasable disagreement between righteousness and iniquity, so long as we remain sinners, he cannot receive us wholly. Therefore, that taking away all manner of disagreement, he might wholly reconcile us unto himself, he doth by expiation set forth in the death of Christ, take away whatsoever evil is in us, that we, who before were unclean and impure, may now appear righteous and holy in his sight." [1]

Since God's love is stronger than His anger, however, He does not destroy the sinner, but has mercy upon him. On the other hand, He does not carelessly overlook sin, but makes satisfaction for it in the death of His Son. It is easy to sneer at this crude conception of an angry God and to compare it unfavourably with a more refined philosophical theory of God. The weight of sin is not considered. At the Cradle and at the Cross of Christ we stand in the presence of something happening to God, to sin and to ourselves. And though our words of the anger of God and the repentance of God are the stammerings of fools, say them we must unless we would take Christ out of His Cradle and down from His Cross. "For God was in Christ reconciling the world unto Himself." Calvin cannot, therefore, interpret the life and acts of Jesus as other than the activity of God. The "hour" of the cross was "not an hour which is determined by the fancy of men, but an hour which God had appointed". [2] For "we ought always to remember, that the wicked executioners of Christ did nothing but what had been determined by the hand and purpose of God; but God did not surrender His Son to their lawless passions, but determined that according to His own will and good pleasure, He should be offered as a sacrifice. And if there were the best reasons for the purpose of God in all those things which He determined that His Son should suffer, we ought to consider on the one hand, the dreadful weight of His wrath against us, and on the other hand, His infinite goodness towards us". [3]

[1] *Inst.* II. xvi. 3. C.R. II, pp. 369–70.
[2] *In Joann.* 17. 1. C.R. XLVII, p. 375. C.T.S. II, p. 164.
[3] *In Joann.* 19. 18. C.R. XLVII, p. 414. C.T.S. II, p. 226.

But Christ was not a passive instrument of the purpose of God. In that there would have been no redemptive value. Our redemption comes from His obedience to the will of His Father— in the vivid phrase of Professor D. M. Mackinnon, "this astounding obliteration of self-will". [1] "Now, in answer to the inquiry how Christ has destroyed the enmity between God and us by the abolition of our sins, and procured a righteousness to render Him favourable and propitious to us, it may be replied in general, that He accomplished it for us by the whole course of His obedience." [2] Karl Barth has criticised *Le Catéchisme de Genève* for its minimising of the life-story of Jesus: "In his Catechism of 1545 Calvin at this passage of the symbol makes the teacher put the following question to the scholar: 'Why do you pass immediately from His birth to His death, and skip the rest of His life-story?' . . . But the answer also, which, according to Calvin's Catechism, the scholar has to give to this question, cannot be described as satisfactory. It runs: 'Here (i.e. in the Creed) there is mentioned only what belongs to the real substance of our Redemption'. . . . Calvin's living pupils, namely, the authors of the Heidelberg Catechism, saw in this case not only more deeply, but above all more correctly from a Biblical-exegetical point of view than their Master when at the corresponding place (Q. 37) in answer to the question, 'What do you understand by the Word, *suffered?*' they said, 'That *all the time He lived on earth, but especially at the end of His life*, He bore, in body and soul, the wrath of God against the sin of the whole human race". [3]

The criticism is just—of the *Catechism*. But the *Catechism* does not in this matter fully reveal Calvin's mind—as Dr. Barth ought to have mentioned. Calvin also regarded the whole course of the life of Jesus as redemptive. Thus, in the *Institutio* he says: "Which is proved by the testimonies of Paul: 'As by one man's offence many were made sinners, so by one man's obedience we are made righteous.' And in another place he extends the cause of the pardon which exempts us from the curse of the Law to the whole life of Christ. 'When the fullness of the time

---

[1] Review of *God Was In Christ*, by D. M. Baillie, in *Scottish Journal of Theology*, vol. 1, no. 2, p. 208.
[2] *Inst.* II. xvi. 5. C.R. II, pp. 370–71.
[3] *Credo*. (Eng. Trans. by J. S. Macnab. London, 1936), p. 73.

was come, God sent forth His Son, made of a woman, made under the law, to redeem them that were under the law.' Thus He affirmed that even in His baptism was fulfilled one part of righteousness, because He acted in obedience to the command of the Father. In short, from the time of His assuming the character of a servant, He began to pay the price of our deliverance in order to redeem us". [1] He then goes on to amplify the teaching of the *Catechism:* "Yet more precisely to define the means of our salvation, the Scripture ascribes it in a particular way to the death of Christ . . . Wherefore, in what is called the Apostle's Creed, there is very properly an immediate transition from the birth of Christ to His death and resurrection, in which the sum of perfect salvation consists. Yet there is no exclusion of the rest of the obedience which He performed in His life". [2] Calvin thus regards the death of Christ as the *summa*, the intensive focal point, of His life; and hence places the emphasis upon it, but comprehending and not excluding the rest of His life and actions.

The obedience of Christ is the meaning of His humiliation and suffering. It is that humiliation born of obedience which is the *exhibitio gratiae Dei*, the revelation of the grace of God. And this humiliation must be regarded as the revelation, not only of God's *kindness* towards us (e.g. to what lengths would He not go for us?) but of His mercy: "by that humiliation He exhibits the infinite goodness of God". [3] The suffering of Christ means, then, that God did not leave us to perish in our sins, when He might very well have done so, but sends Christ to save us from our sins. It means at the same time that Christ has been freely obedient to the will of God, and so has reconciled us to God. In Him, the obedient representative of mankind, God has judged and forgiven us.

The revelation of the Father in Jesus is not the revelation of a fatherly character called God, but the revelation of mercy, forgiveness and adoption by which we are brought from enmity towards God to be the dear children of a gracious and almighty Father. We can take this most intimate name upon our lips and

[1] *Inst.* II. xvi. 5. C.R. II, p. 371.
[2] *Inst.* II. xvi. 5. C.R. II, p. 371.
[3] *In Joann.* 14. 9. C.R. XLVII, p. 326. C.T.S. II, p. 87.

say "Our Father," because in Christ our prodigality is pardoned and we are brought back to our origin, to fellowship with God. "We cannot, from a contemplation of the world, conclude that He is our Father, when our conscience disturbs us within, and convinces us that our sins afford a just reason why God should abandon us and no longer regard us as His children. . . . Wherefore, though the preaching of the cross is not agreeable to human reason, we ought nevertheless to embrace it with all humility, if we desire to return to God our Creator, from whom we have been alienated, and to have Him re-assume the character of our Father." [1]

"If we seek salvation, we are taught by the name of *Jesus*, that it is in Him; if we seek any other gifts of the Spirit, they will be found in His unction; strength, in His dominion; purity, in His conception; indulgence shows itself in His nativity, by which He was made to resemble us in all things, that He might learn to condole with us; if we seek redemption, it will be found in His passion; absolution, in His condemnation; remission of the curse, in His cross; satisfaction, in His sacrifice; purification, in His blood; reconciliation, in His descent into hell; mortification of the flesh, in His sepulchre; newness of life and immortality, in His resurrection; the inheritance of the celestial kingdom, in His entrance into heaven; protection, security, abundance, and enjoyment of all blessings, in His kingdom; a fearless expectation of the judgement, in the judicial authority committed to Him. Finally, blessings of every kind are deposited in Him; let us draw from His treasury, and from no other source, till our desires are satisfied." [2]

[1]*Inst.* II. vi. 1. C.R. II, p. 247.
[2]*Inst.* II. xvi. 19. C.R. II, pp. 385–6.

CHAPTER SIX

THE KNOWLEDGE OF CHRIST

1

BY CHRIST-MAN TO CHRIST-GOD

God, the incomprehensible and hidden, has revealed Himself
to us in Jesus Christ, and, apart from Him, remains hidden and
incomprehensible to us. Hence we must "see" Christ in order
that we may see God; we must know Christ that we may know
God. "Since God 'dwelleth in the light, which no man can
approach unto,' there is need of the interposition of Christ, as the
medium of access to Him. Whence He calls Himself 'the light of
the world,' and in another place, 'the way, and the truth, and the
life' because 'no man cometh unto the Father,' who is the
fountain of life, 'but by Him;' for He alone knows the Father
and reveals Him to believers. . . . It is true that faith relates to
the one God, but there must also be added a knowledge of Jesus
Christ, whom He has sent. For God Himself would be altogether
concealed from us, if we were not illuminated by the brightness
of Christ. For this purpose the Father has deposited all His
treasures with His only-begotten Son, that He might reveal
Himself in Him; and that, by such a communication of blessings,
He might express a true image of His glory. For, as it has been
observed that we need to be drawn by the Spirit so that we may
be moved to seek Christ, so we should also be apprised that the
invisible Father is to be sought only in this image." [1] In what
this seeing and knowing consists is the object of our inquiry in
this chapter.

It will be remembered that in our previous chapter we saw
that one meaning of the Incarnation of the Son of God was that
He was God come near to man, *Emmanuel.* The proximity of
God in Christ tells us that in Christ God comes even within our
ken, that the boundary between God and man has been crossed—
by God. G. K. Chesterton, in his little book on St. Francis of
Assisi formulates the astounding theory that Christ Himself is at
a distance from us, but St. Francis, as the mirror of Christ,

[1] *Inst.* III. ii. 1. C.R. II, p. 398.

brings Him near to us, within our experience: "St. Francis is the mirror of Christ rather as the moon is the mirror of the sun. The moon is much smaller than the sun, but it is also much nearer to us; and being less vivid, it is more visible. Exactly in the same sense St. Francis is nearer to us, and being a mere man like ourselves is in that sense more imaginable".[1] This is high Christology run to seed, and a good example of what Calvin called "obscuring Christ". Jesus of Nazareth is very man. If He were not, He could not be the mirror of God to man. But God shines in Him and He shines forth to men. It is with the humanity of Christ that we must begin, says Calvin, and so rise to His Deity: "for the reason why Christ descended to us, and first was humbled and afterwards was placed at the Father's right hand, and obtained dominion over heaven and earth, was that He might exalt us to His own divine glory, and to the glory of the Father. That our faith may arrive at the eternal Divinity of Christ, we must begin with that knowledge which is nearer and more easily acquired. Thus it has been justly said by some, that by Christ Man we are conducted to Christ God, because our faith makes such gradual progress that, perceiving Christ on earth, born in a stable, and hanging on a cross, it rises to the glory of His resurrection, and proceeding onwards, comes at length to His eternal life and power, in which His Divine majesty is gloriously displayed".[2]

In all our thinking about God, in all our coming to God in confession, worship, prayer and thanksgiving, we should come through Jesus Christ; that is, through this particular historical figure. And in all our thoughts of the Second Person of the Trinity, we should begin, not with the *aeternus Sermo Dei*, who is no less hidden from us than the Father and the Spirit, but with the man, Jesus of Nazareth, to whose existence, acts and suffer-

---

[1] *St. Francis of Assisi.* (Black Jacket Edn. London, 1946), p. 140.

[2] *In Joann.* 20. 28. C.R. XLVII, p. 444. C.T.S. II, p. 277. Cf. Luther: "Wherefore whensoever thou art occupied in the matter of thy salvation, setting aside all curious speculations of God's unsearchable Majesty, all cogitations of works, of traditions, of Philosophy, yea, of God's law too, run straight to the manger and embrace this infant, and the Virgine's little babe in thine armes, and behold him as he was borne, sucking, growing up, conversant among men, teaching, dying, rising againe, ascending up above all the heavens, and having power above all things. . . . And this sight and contemplation will keepe thee in the right way, that thou maist follow whither Christ is gone." (*Comm. in Gal.* W. A. 40 : 1, pp. 79–80. E. T., p. 17 b.)

G

ings we give that special significance which is the substance of the Christian faith. "And, indeed, if this were deeply impressed on the hearts of all, that the Son of God holds out to us the hand of a brother, and that we are united to Him by the fellowship of our nature, so that, out of our lowly condition, He may raise us to Heaven, who would not choose to keep to this straight road, instead of wandering in uncertain and stormy paths? Accordingly, whenever in our praying to God we remember that exalted and unapproachable majesty, let us at the same time, that we may not be driven back by the dread of it, remember the man Christ who gently invites us, and takes us, as it were, by the hand, so that the Father, who had been the object of terror and alarm, may be reconciled by Him and rendered friendly to us." [1]

But the way to the knowledge of God is by the revelation of the whole Godhead: "to the Father is attributed the principle of action, the fountain and source of all things; to the Son, wisdom, counsel and the dispensation of all operations; and the power and efficacy of the action is assigned to the Spirit". [2] To separate the Spirit from the work of the Son, and to give Him, so to speak, a roving commission in the affairs between God and man, even a commission not most closely related to the work of the Son, is to sunder the simple will of God and to lapse, in effect, into tritheism. The Holy Spirit is the Spirit of Christ: "And it must be remarked, that He is called the Spirit of Christ, not only because the eternal Word of God is united with the same Spirit as the Father, but also with respect to His character as Mediator; for, if He had not been endued with this power, His advent to us would have been altogether in vain". [3] As the Spirit of Christ, working in conjunction with Him in effecting the redeeming will of the Father, His office is to unite men with Christ so that they shall participate in those blessings which He obtained for them by His obedience. That which the Son of God came to do, He accomplished fully and finally, so that in Him all men are saved. But the words *in Him* must be taken seriously. We are

---

[1] *In I Tim.* 2. 5.   C.R. LII, p. 270.   C.T.S., p. 57.
[2] *Inst.* I. xiii. 18.   C.R. II, p. 105.   It was amusing, at the time I wrote this chapter, to read in an article in *Theology* that the Reformers "never came near to reviving the great doctrine of the Holy Spirit." (P. Pare: *The Doctrine of the Holy Spirit in the Western Church. Theology*, August, 1948, p. 296.)
[3] *Inst.* III. i. 2.   C.R. II, p. 395.

not saved by contemplating Christ from a distance, but by being united with Him: "so long as there is separation between Christ and us, all that He suffered and performed for the salvation of mankind is useless and unavailing to us. To communicate to us what He received from His Father, He must, therefore, become ours, and dwell within us". [1]

How are we to understand this union of Christ with men? It is not an achievement of the soul, any more than is the knowledge of God. Just as the *ordo salutis* is from God to man, so it is also from Christ to man. We can no more come uninvited to Christ than we can penetrate the ineffable light in which dwells the Father. "No man can come to me, except the Father, which hath sent me, draw him." [2] "What!" cries Calvin, having quoted this verse, "is He not Himself the lively image of the Father, representing to us all the brightness of His glory? . . . What! did He not descend to the earth in order to reveal to men the will of the Father? And did He not faithfully fulfil the object of His mission? Certainly He did; but His preaching is not at all efficacious unless the way to the heart be laid open by the internal teaching of the Spirit". [3] The union with Christ is effected by the Holy Spirit, not by man himself. "The sum of all is this: that the Holy Spirit is the bond by which Christ efficaciously unites us with Himself." [4] By "this mysterious intercourse which we have with Christ" [5] He becomes ours, and we become His. His properties are given to us and ours to Him. "This union alone renders His advent in the character of a Saviour available to us. We learn the same truth from that sacred marriage whereby we are made flesh of His flesh and bone of His bone, and therefore one with Him. It is only by His Spirit that He unites Himself with us; and by the grace and power of the same Spirit we are made His members, that He may keep us under Himself and we may mutually enjoy Him." [6]

[1] *Inst.* III. i. 1. C.R. II, p. 393.
[2] *John.* 6. 44.
[3] *Inst.* II. ii. 20. C.R. II, p. 202.
[4] *Inst.* III. i. 1. C.R. II, p. 394.
[5] *In Eph.* 5. 29. C.R. LI, p. 225. C.T.S., p. 323.
[6] *Inst.* III. i. 3. C.R. II, p. 396. Nevertheless, Calvin does not bring out so strongly as Luther the intercommunication of properties between Christ and the sinner. Cf. Luther's justly famous letter to Georg Spenlein: "lieber Herr Jesu, du bist meine Gerechtigkeit, ich aber bin deine Sünde. Du hast angenommen, was mein ist, und hast mir gegeben, was dein ist." *Briefe (Weimar Ausgabe)* 1, p. 35.

The Holy Spirit unites us with Christ, and this union is to be conceived of as one of faith, for it is when we believe in Christ that we are one with Him. It is not possible, however, for men to believe in Jesus Christ—that is, to know who He is and therefore what His significance is, and to apprehend Him in trust: *"non sunt idonei homines ad credendum"*.[1] As it was during His life on earth, so it is always. Not all men knew who He was. Rather, no man knew who He was until He revealed Himself to him. For He was hidden from men by those very qualities which were the revelation of the will of God, His humanity and His humility: "for a time His divine glory was invisible, and nothing appeared but the human form".[2] When, however, He so willed, He revealed Himself to certain men and women. And this revelation was by the illumination of the Holy Spirit, who was always in Him during His earthly life. Before His public ministry He had enjoyed His presence as *privatus homo*, but at His baptism He received the Spirit for His public ministry, so that He might, by the power of the Spirit, be known as the Son of God: "For this was done deliberately, so that believers might learn to behold and embrace reverently His divine power: nor was the infirmity of the flesh contemptible in Him. . . . Therefore the Holy Spirit descending upon Christ appeared to John to teach him that nothing carnal or earthly is to be sought in that same Christ, but that He is, as it were, the Divine man coming forth from heaven, in whom reigns the power of the Holy Spirit".[3] It is by the power of the Holy Spirit, then, that Jesus Christ reveals Himself and so reveals God.

The revelation of Christ is not only subjective, however, but also objective in the same act of revelation. When He revealed Himself, He was known to the recipients of the revelation, and that, not by natural apprehension, but by the supernatural illumination of the Spirit. The revelation and the perception of the revelation are not two closely related activities of the Holy Spirit, but one activity whereby revelation occurs and is known to be revelation. The unity of this action becomes more apparent if, instead of revelation, we speak of Christ making Himself

[1] *Inst.* III. ii. 35. C.R. II, p. 427.
[2] *Inst.* II. xiii. 2. C.R. II, p. 349.
[3] *In Matt.* 3. 16. C.R. XLV, p. 126. C.T.S. I, p. 204.

known to us. Both the subjective and objective sides of revelation are comprehended in this one action, which is the work of the Holy Spirit.

When men are confronted by Jesus of Nazareth they are able not to believe in Him. They can disbelieve His witness concerning Himself, and they can find a natural explanation of His miracles. All this because they are blind to Him and see Him as other than the Son of God. To see Him as He is, the illumination of the Holy Spirit, which is revelation, must be given to them. When, however, they are enlightened by the Spirit, they acknowledge the claims of Christ, recognizing Him to be the Son of God, and if the Incarnate Son of God, then come into the world to be their Redeemer. In other words, by the *illuminatio Spiritus sancti* they *know* Christ, and that not with a theoretical knowledge, but with an empirical, a knowledge which is union, and if union, then participation in all that Christ is and has.

2

THE MEDIA OF KNOWLEDGE

It is still necessary for us, if we would know God, to know Christ; to know of Him, to hear Him, to see His miracles. Obviously, this can only be at second-hand, by means of the gospel records—those four horses drawing the chariot in which Christ rides in magnificence, as Calvin quaintly puts it. That the gospels are a second-hand record of Jesus Christ does not, however, derogate from their importance as a link in the chain of revelation; for in the first place, Calvin holds that they are a true record, wherein we see the authentic figure of Jesus—authentic both historically and also theologically; and secondly, they are not a mere recitation of the facts of His life, but by the power of the Holy Spirit they themselves become to us the revelation of Jesus Christ. This is, however, true, not only of the four gospels, but of the Gospel itself, wherever it is found.

"But that seeing, of which Christ now speaks, has been enjoyed by believers in every age in common with the Apostles. We do not see Christ—and yet we do see Him. We do not hear

Christ—and yet we do hear Him. For in the Gospel we behold Him, as Paul says, face to face, so as to be transformed into His image, and the perfection and wisdom, righteousness and life which was formerly exhibited in Him, shines there continually." [1]

"True, Christ no longer dwells on earth, nor do we carry Him in our arms [as Simeon did]; but His divine majesty shines openly and brightly in the Gospel, and there do 'we all,' as Paul says, 'behold as in a glass the glory of the Lord,' not, as formerly, amidst the weakness of the flesh, but in the glorious power of the Spirit, which He displayed in His miracles, in the sacrifice of His death, and in His resurrection." [2]

"There were many unbelievers who, at that time, beheld Christ with the eyes of the flesh, and yet were not more blessed on that account; but we, who have never seen Christ with our eyes, enjoy that blessedness of which Christ speaks with commendation.   Hence it follows, that He calls those eyes blessed which spiritually behold in Him what is heavenly and divine; for we now behold Christ in the Gospel in the same manner as if He visibly stood before us." [3]

But Calvin's use of the word *Gospel* is at first sight somewhat confusing.   He speaks very frequently, of course, of "the preaching of the Gospel," but this does not cover all its meanings. What does he mean, for example, when he says that we must receive Christ "invested with His Gospel"? [4] What, again, is the relationship between Bible and Gospel?

The Gospel is, first, the New Covenant promised in Jeremiah 31. 31f and fulfilled in Jesus Christ. This is the tenor of *Institutio* II. xi, where he uses Old Testament interchangeably with Law and New Testament with Gospel: "The three last comparisons which we have mentioned are between the Law and the Gospel. In these, therefore, the Old Testament denotes the Law, and the New Testament the Gospel". [5] So also in the *Commentary on Galations* 4. 22ff: "As in the house of Abraham there were two mothers, so are there also in the Church of God. Doctrine is the mother of which we are born, and is twofold, Legal and Evan-

[1]*In Matt.* 13. 16. C.R. XLV, p. 362. C.T.S. II, p. 110.
[2]*In Luc.* 2. 30. C.R. XLV, p. 90. C.T.S. I, p. 144.
[3]*In Joann.* 20. 29. C.R. XLVII, pp. 445-6. C.T.S. II, p. 279.
[4]*Inst.* III. ii. 6. C.R. II, p. 401.
[5]*Inst.* II. xi. 10. C.R. II, p. 336.

gelical". [1] The Gospel is, then, the New Covenant, consisting in "repentance and remission of sins". [2]

Secondly, the Gospel is the declaration of the New Covenant in Jesus Christ: *"Ergo Euangelium solennis est promulgatio de Filio Dei in carne exhibito, ut perditum mundum instauret, ac homines restituat ex morte in vitam"*. [3] It is "a clear manifestation of the mystery of Christ"; [4] "the promulgation of the grace exhibited in Christ;" [5] and "the lively exhibition of those things". [6] It is "the appointed preaching of Christ as manifested". [7]

Concerning this there are two questions to be asked: First; in what does this promulgation, manifestation, exhibition or preaching consist? Secondly; what is its relationship to the revelation and knowledge of God in Christ?

The preaching of the Gospel is two-fold; in the Scriptures and by the Church. Not all the Scripture is Gospel. The Law and its attendant curses are not Gospel, for example. Parts of the Old Testament, however, may be called Gospel, since it includes promises of grace as well as the Law: "I grant indeed, since Paul calls the Gospel *the doctrine of faith*, that whatever promises we find in the Law concerning the gracious remission of sins, by which God reconciles men to Himself, are accounted parts of it. For he opposes faith to those terrors which torment and harass the conscience, if salvation is to be sought by works. Whence it follows that, taking the word *Gospel* in a broad sense, it comprehends all those testimonies, which God formerly gave to the patriarchs, of His mercy and paternal favour; but it is more eminently applicable to the promulgation of the grace exhibited in Christ". [8] The promises in the Old Testament, however, can hardly be said to belong to the Old Covenant, but to the New, for the substance of the promises was Christ, who was also the substance of the New Covenant. Thus, commenting on the verse, "to Abraham and to his seed were the promises made," he

---

[1] *In Gal.* 4. 24. C.R. L, p. 237. C.T.S., p. 137.
[2] *Inst.* III. iii. 1. C.R. II, p. 434.
[3] *Arg. to Comm. on Harm. of Gosp.* C.R. XLV, p. 2. C.T.S. I, p. xxxvi.
[4] *Inst.* II. ix. 2. C.R. II, p. 310.
[5] Ibid. C.R. II, p. 310.
[6] Ibid. C.R. II, p. 311.
[7] *In Rom.* 1. 2. C.R. XLIX, p. 9. C.T.S., p. 43.
[8] *Inst.* II. ix. 2. C.R. II, p. 310.

says: "But if Christ be the foundation of the Covenant, it follows that it is of free grace; and this, too, is the meaning of the word *promise*. As the Law has respect to men and to their works, so the promise has respect to the grace of God and to faith". [1] The promulgation of the Gospel is thus those promises in the Bible relating to the forgiveness of sins and eternal life in Jesus Christ. And since they are there set out more clearly, because Christ had been manifested in the flesh, particularly the promises in the New Testament.

The promulgation of the Gospel is also the preaching of the Church: "as often as Christ calls us to the hope of salvation by the preaching of the Gospel, He is present with us. For not without reason is the preaching of the Gospel called Christ's descent to us". [2] This preaching consists in words and activities, that is, in sermons, and, indeed, in any verbal and literary form, and in the Sacraments, which not only, on account of man's obtuseness, support and confirm oral preaching, but are also a form of preaching themselves, in that they show forth the will of God in Christ. Thus Calvin calls the Eucharist "*un miroir auquel nous contemplions nostre Seigneur Iesus crucifié pour abolir noz faultes et offences, et resuscité pour nous delivrer de corruption et de mort, nous restituant en immortalité celeste*". [3] The promulgation of the Gospel is, however, only the preaching of the Church when that preaching is a loyal expression of the Scriptural promulgation of the Gospel. When the Church indulges in her own "*songes et resveries*", she is not preaching the Gospel.

Now, what is the relationship between the Gospel of which we have been speaking and the revelation and knowledge of God in Jesus Christ?

We must refer back at this stage to our discussion of Calvin's doctrine of the Word of God. "Therefore, as all Divine revela-

[1] *In Gal.* 3. 16. C.R. L, p. 211. C.T.S., p. 94. The Lutheran position was very similar. Thus Melanchthon says: "Nor has the Scripture so narrated law and gospel in such a manner that one would regard as gospel what Matthew, Mark, Luke and John have written, and as law what Moses has recorded. But the plan of the gospel is scattered; there are promises in both the Old and New Testaments." (*Loci Communes*, 1521 Edn. C.R. XXI, p. 139. Eng. Trans. by C. L. Hill, Boston, Mass. 1944, p. 144.) And Luther: "Just so in the Old Testament there are, besides the Laws, certain promises and offers of grace, by which the holy fathers and prophets under the law, were kept, like us, under the faith of Christ." Deutsche Bibel (W. A.) V, p. 3.
[2] *In Joann.* 7. 33. C.R. XLVII, p. 178. C.T.S. I, p. 303.
[3] *Petit Traicté de la Saincte Cene.* C.R. V, p. 437.

tions are justly entitled *verbum Dei*," says Calvin, "so we ought
chiefly to esteem that substantial Word the source of all revelations, who is liable to no variation, who remains with God
perpetually one and the same, and who is God Himself". [1] But
he also calls the Scriptures *verbum* or *Sermo Dei*, and the preaching of the Gospel as well; thus: "*Nam sermo pro Euangelii
doctrina capitur*". [2] Moreover, the promulgation of the Gospel in
Scripture and in preaching is not called *the Word of God* in any
loose sense or apart from the general meaning outlined previously. The term is meant to carry its precise and real meaning.
The proclamation of the Gospel is the Word of God as really as
those *oracula Dei* spoken to the patriarchs and prophets. So he
says of the Scriptures: "But since we are not favoured with daily
oracles from heaven, and since it is only in the Scriptures that the
Lord has been pleased to preserve His truth in perpetual remem-
brance, it obtains the same credit and authority with believers
when they are satisfied of its Divine origin, as if they heard the
very words pronounced by God Himself." [3] And of the preaching of the Church: "Especially it is said: 'The people has been
rebellious against the mouth of God.' But why is that? It does
not say that God appeared in a visible form, or that a voice from
the sky had been heard. No, it was Moses who had spoken; it
was a man who said that the people had resisted the mouth of
God. So we see how God wishes His Word to be received in
such humility when He sends men to declare what He commands
them, as if He were in the midst of us. The teaching, then, which
is put forward in the name of God, ought to be as authoritative
as if all the angels of heaven descended to us, as if God Himself
had revealed His majesty before our eyes". [4] It is true that, so
far at least as preaching is concerned, the words of the preacher
must not be taken to be synonymous with the Word of God.
The distinction between God and man must not be blurred. The
fact that preaching may be the Word of God Himself is utterly
and entirely of the gracious will of God.

As, however, I have dealt with Calvin's doctrine of preaching
at some length in my book on his preaching, it is unnecessary to

[1] *Inst.* I. xiii. 7. C.R. II, p. 95.
[2] *In Joann.* 17. 17. C.R. XLVII, p. 381. C.T.S. II, p. 180.
[3] *Inst.* I. vii. 1. C.R. II, p. 56.
[4] *Sermon on Deuteronomy.* C.R. XXV, p. 713.

be detailed here, and perhaps I may be allowed to refer to the exposition given there, and here merely set out the findings: (1) "Preaching is the Word of God, first, in the sense that it is an exposition and interpretation of the Bible." [1] (2) "Preaching is the Word of God because the preacher has been sent and commissioned by God as His ambassador, the one who has authority to speak in His name." [2] (3) "Preaching is the Word of God in the sense that it is Revelation." [3] And this last, not because of any virtue inherent in preaching itself, which is merely a human activity, but because "preaching *becomes* Revelation by God adding to it His Holy Spirit". [4]

As the Word of God, therefore, the proclamation of the Gospel in Scripture and the preaching of the Church is the revelation of God. It is revelation, not because man reveals God to man, but because God reveals Himself in it. This is not precise enough, however. The Gospel is "*solennis promulgatio de Filio Dei in carne exhibito,*" and this same Son of God manifested in the flesh is the revelation of God. Moreover, it was by the Holy Spirit that He made Himself known, and it is by the power of the Holy Spirit that the words of men become the Word of God. The Gospel is, then, God's self-manifestation in Jesus Christ by the Holy Spirit. It is an integral part of the Divine purpose of redemption.

By the Gospel we know God. But we do not understand and receive the Gospel by natural apprehension, for "we are all blind by nature". We need the illumination of the Holy Spirit so that we may understand and embrace it. The Holy Spirit, when He makes the proclamation of the Gospel into revelation, enlightens our minds to understand and gives us obedience to submit to the teaching of the Gospel. To submit to the Gospel is to submit our intellects to the wisdom of God, and to acknowledge that we do not know God and are unable to know Him by ourselves, and therefore need to be taught. Reason is not discarded but dethroned; wisdom is discarded. "Human sagacity is here so completely lost, that the first step to improvement in the Divine school, is to forsake it. For like an interposing

[1] *The Oracles of God.* (London, 1947), p. 50.
[2] Ibid., p. 51.
[3] Ibid., p. 53.
[4] Ibid., p. 55.

veil it prevents us from discovering the mysteries of God, which are revealed only to babes . . . Therefore, as we can never come to Christ unless we are drawn by the Spirit of God, so when we are drawn, we are raised both in mind and in heart above the reach of our own understanding. For, illuminated by Him, the soul receives, as it were, new eyes for the contemplation of heavenly mysteries, by the splendour of which it was before dazzled. And thus the human intellect, irradiated by the light of the Holy Spirit, then begins to relish those things which pertain to the kingdom of God, for which before it had not the slightest taste." [1]

Concretely, the Word as the object of faith means that God reveals Himself, and therefore that we know Him by faith, in the promulgation of the Gospel in the Bible and in the preaching of the Church. God comes to us and makes Himself known to us as our Father in Christ when we read, hear, or meditate upon the Scriptures and preaching, when we meditate on our baptism, when we receive the Body and Blood of Christ in the Eucharist. These things, says Calvin, become to us the *speculum Dei*, in which we behold the image of God, the *effigies Dei*. "The ministry of the Word, I say, is like a mirror. For the angels have no need of preaching, or other inferior aids, nor of sacraments, for they enjoy a vision of God of another kind; and God does not give them a view of His face merely in a mirror, but openly manifests Himself as present with them. We, who have not as yet reached that great height, behold the image of God as it is presented before us in the Word, in the sacraments, and in fine, in the whole service of the Church." [2]

[1] *Inst.* III. ii. 34. C.R. II, pp. 426–7.
[2] *In I Cor.* 13. 12. C.R. XLIX, p. 514. C.T.S. I, p. 430.

CHAPTER SEVEN

THE KNOWLEDGE OF FAITH

FROM the earliest days of the Church the connection between knowledge and faith had been recognized. The Fathers had strong Johannine influence to guide them on the one side, and on the other, the entry of Hellenistic philosophy into the Church through the Apologists and Alexandrians brought the concept of knowledge to the front, where it had to be reconciled with the foremost Christian idea, that of faith. This attempt at reconciliation constitutes the chief aim of Clement of Alexandria. For him the summit is the knowledge of God, and the advanced Christian is he who has passed by way of faith into knowledge; he is the Gnostic, the knower, and, as such, a spiritual aristocrat. But the important point to notice at the moment is that Clement does so connect faith and knowledge: "Now neither is knowledge without faith, nor faith without knowledge". [1] So also Cyril of Jerusalem: "Faith is an eye that enlightens every conscience, and imparts understanding". [2] So also Augustine: "We believed that we might know; for if we wished first to know and then to believe, we should not be able either to know or to believe". [3] Faith was related to knowledge but not identified with it. It was fairly generally agreed that faith precedes knowledge, but within this order there was ample scope for variety of interpretation. For Clement, as we have said, faith is merely the entrance to knowledge, with which he is principally interested: "And, in truth, faith is discovered by us to be the first movement towards salvation; after which fear, and hope, and repentance, advancing in company with temperance and patience, lead us to love and knowledge". [4] For Augustine also, as in the passage quoted, faith precedes knowledge; but he does not contrast them sharply like Clement, but rather regards them as complementary. Nor does knowledge make faith superfluous, for knowledge in this life is always a knowledge of faith. Mr. J. Burnaby says that,

[1] *Stromata.* V. 1.
[2] *Catechetical Lectures.* V. 4.
[3] *In Joann. Evang.* 27. 9.
[4] *Stromata* II. 4.

for Augustine, "There is no opposition between faith and understanding: the highest gifts of understanding do not make faith
superfluous. But faith and vision are contraries which exclude
one another". [1]

The schoolmen still adhered to this connection of faith and
knowledge and the traditional order of faith-knowledge, which
Anselm, echoing Augustine, set in his classic phrase *"Credo, ut
intelligam"*. Indeed, this connection and order are so general
that Professor Gilson can say: "There is no question of
maintaining—no one has ever maintained—that faith is a
kind of cognition superior to rational cognition. It is quite
clear, on the contrary, that belief is a succedaneum of knowledge, and that to substitute science for belief, wherever
possible, is always a positive gain for the understanding. For
Christian thinkers the traditional hierarchy of the modes of
cognition is always faith, understanding and vision of God face
to face". [2]

When we come to Calvin, we find as usual that he stands
within the tradition of the Church. He thinks not only Biblically
but traditionally. In this matter he does not depart from the
customary connection (which is everywhere apparent) or order. [3]
"And have believed. Let it be observed, also, he employs the
verb *know*, and now he uses the verb *believe;* for thus he shows
that nothing which relates to God can be known aright but by
faith, but that in faith there is such certainty that it is justly called
knowledge." [4] "It was the Apostle's intention to explain what is
the nature of true faith, and in what it consists; that is, when
the Son of God is known." [5] Yet he shows some significant
differences from the past, chiefly in two directions: he binds
faith and knowledge in an even closer connection; and although,

---

[1] *Amor Dei: A Study of the Religion of St. Augustine.* (London, 1938), p. 75.
[2] *The Spirit of Mediaeval Philosophy*, p. 35.
[3] Calvin was, of course, far from being in agreement with all that had been
held by representative theologians about the substance of knowledge. For example, although, broadly speaking, he keeps to Gilson's "traditional hierarchy"
of "faith, understanding and vision of God", his concept of understanding
differs quite radically from the Thomist. For Thomism, the knowledge of
God is a part of epistemology; i.e. it is a part of our general knowledge and differs
from other sorts of knowledge in that its object is different. For Calvin, however,
the knowing itself differs from general knowing.
[4] *In Joann.* 17. 8. C.R. XLVII, p. 380. C.T.S. II, p. 172.
[5] *In Eph.* 4. 13. C.R. LI, p. 200. C.T.S., p. 283.

like Augustine, faith has a strong intellectual emphasis for him, he regards knowledge as faith, rather than faith as direct knowledge.

For him the two concepts are inter-related, so that there is between them a sort of mutual precedence and generation. Sometimes he will speak of knowledge producing faith: "The commencement of faith is knowledge". [1] Or: "Moreover, these words show that faith proceeds from the knowledge of Christ". [2] Elsewhere he speaks of faith producing knowledge: "The word *believe* is put first, because the obedience of faith is the commencement of right understanding". [3] This apparent contradiction is resolved by the fact that he uses *knowledge* in two senses; sometimes, but by no means always, employing two different words. The knowledge that precedes and produces faith is, in the given quotations, *notitia*. That which follows faith is *cognitio*. He also uses *scientia* for *cognitio*. In the following passage this careful use of words (which we could wish he had everywhere observed), shows quite clearly his mind on the relation of *notitia—fides—cognitio:* "Although he places faith after knowledge (*scientia*), as if it were inferior, he does so because he has to do with unbelieving and obstinate men, who never yield to God until they are vanquished and constrained by experience; for rebels wish to know (*scire*) before they believe. And yet our gracious God indulges us so far, that He prepares us for faith by a knowledge (*notitia*) of His works. But the knowledge of God (*cognitio Dei*) and of His secret wisdom comes after faith, because the obedience of faith opens to us the door of the kingdom of heaven." [4]

There is, then, according to Calvin, a certain knowledge which precedes and begets faith; which is, indeed, a *praeparatio fidei*. It is very important that we should ask in what this *notitia* consists, and in what sense it is a preparation for faith. We can rule out at once the idea that it is in any way an inherent knowledge of God. It is not the *sensus Deitatis* with which man is naturally endued, for that is either stifled at its inception or produces only superstition. Nor is it that *praeparatio Euangelii*

[1] *In Eph.* 1. 13. C.R. LI, p. 153. C.T.S., p. 208.
[2] *In Joann.* 6. 40. C.R. XLVII, p. 148. C.T.S. I, p. 255.
[3] *In Joann.* 6. 69. C.R. XLVII, p. 163. C.T.S. I, p. 279.
[4] *In Joann.* 10. 38. C.R. XLVII, p. 254. C.T.S. I, p. 422.

of which the Apologists were so enamoured. "I do not deny,"
says Calvin, "that some judicious and apposite observations
concerning God may be found scattered in the writings of the
philosophers; but they always betray a confused imagination. . . .
Human reason, then, neither approaches, nor tends, nor directs
its views towards this truth, to understand who is the true God
(*quis sit verus Deus*), or what He wishes to be towards us (*qualisve
erga nos esse velit*)." [1] It is, in fact, not a natural knowledge at all:
"Away now with those who idly say that men are prepared for
receiving the grace of God by the movement of nature. They
might as well say that the dead walk!" [2] Nor is the *notitia Dei*
the knowledge of God the Creator gained from His works
(though, certainly, at first view the passage seems to say this).
For the revelation in the *opera Dei* serves only, as we saw in
Chapter Two, to make men inexcusable. This, indeed, is a sort
of preparation for faith, but it cannot be called a positive
preparation, nor indeed a true knowledge.

The *operum suorum notitia* of the *Commentary on John* 10. 38 is
the sensible cognition of miracles performed by Jesus Christ
resulting in the belief that they were miracles, wrought by "the
finger of God". This is the meaning of *works* in all this passage.
He says the same thing in connection with Nicodemus: "In a
word, as miracles have a two-fold advantage, to prepare the
mind for faith, and, when it has been formed by the Word, to
confirm it still more, Nicodemus had profited aright in the
former part, because by miracles he recognizes Christ as a true
prophet of God". [3] The idea comes also in the *Institutio:* "We
may also style that a *fides implicita*, which in strict propriety is
nothing but a preparation for faith. The evangelists relate that
many believed, who, being merely filled with wonder at the
miracles of Christ, proceeded no further than a persuasion that
He was the promised Messiah, although they had little or no
knowledge of the teaching of the Gospel". [4] Might we perhaps
go further, and say that this *notitia* is the seeing or knowing
Jesus of Nazareth? That is, that it is the first step in the ascent
from Christ-Man to Christ-God?

[1]*Inst.* II. ii. 18. C.R. II, pp. 200–201.
[2]*In Joann.* 11. 25. C.R. XLVII, p. 262. C.T.S. I, p. 435.
[3]*In Joann.* 3. 2. C.R. XLVII, p. 53. C.T.S. I, p. 106.
[4]*Inst.* III. ii. 5. C.R. II, p. 400.

Fides precedes and produces *cognitio*. But we have not
finished with Calvin's doctrine of faith and knowledge by saying,
"*Credo, ut intelligam*". The theme of his chapter on faith is that
"Faith consists in the knowledge of God and of Christ". [1] We
must ask precisely what he intends as the object of knowledge in
the phrase *cognitio Dei*. He does not mean a knowledge of God's
essential Being, or, in the words of *Institutio* I. ii. 2, "*quid sit
Deus*", for such knowledge is an impossibility on earth. He is
here perhaps deliberately drawing upon St. Thomas, who also
held (in opposition to St. Bonaventure and the neo-Platonist
schoolmen) that this knowledge is not possible *in via*. Although
St. Thomas begins Question II of the *Summa Theologica* with
the words "Because the chief aim of sacred doctrine is to teach
the knowledge of God, not only as He is in Himself, but also as
He is the beginning of things and their last end . . ." [2] yet he is
careful to insist that "in this life", even after the revelation of
grace, "we cannot know of God *what He is* (*quid est*), and thus
are united to Him as to one unknown". [3] Not *cognitio quiddita-
tiva*, says St. Thomas. Not *quid sit Deus?* says Calvin, but *qualis
sit Deus?* "Cold and frivolous, then, are the speculations of those
who busy themselves with the question, *quid sit Deus;* when it is
more important for us to know *qualis sit*, and what accords with
His nature." [4] "*Qualis sit, et quid eius naturae conveniat*" must
be interpreted from the context as the manward attitude or will
of God, for Calvin goes on: "For what end is answered by
professing with Epicurus, that there is a God, who discarding all
concern about the world, indulges Himself in perpetual inactivity? What benefit arises from the knowledge of a God with whom
we have no concern?" [5] Thus, with respect to the knowledge of
God the Creator, the answer to *qualis sit Deus?* is "Guardian and
Protector", "the Author of all blessings", "Lord and Father",
"the righteous Judge". [6] These correspond to the *virtutes Dei*
which are the content of the revelation of the Creator: that is,
God's *sapientia, bonitas, potentia*, etc. By these *virtutes* we see

[1] *Inst.* III. ii. 5. C.R. II, p. 399.
[2] *Summa Theologica* Qu. II.
[3] *Summa Theologica* Qu. XII. Art. 13.
[4] *Inst.* I. ii. 2. C.R. II, pp. 34–5.
[5] *Inst.* I. ii. 2. C.R. II, p. 35.
[6] *Inst.* I. ii. 2. C.R. II, p. 35.

what God is like towards us, not what He is in Himself—*"non quis sit apud se, sed qualis erga nos."* [1]

This is true also of the *cognitio Dei redemptoris.* The object of our knowledge is not God in His essence, but God's will towards us. "For the apprehension of faith is not confined to our knowing that there is a God, but chiefly consists in our understanding what is His will towards us. For it is not of so much importance for us to know what He is in Himself (*quis in se sit*), as what He is willing to be to us (*qualis esse nobis velit*). We find, therefore, that faith is a knowledge of the will of God towards us, received from His Word." [2]

But, says Calvin, we must be more precise than that, for not all knowledge of God's will can truly be called the knowledge of God, which is nothing less than the perfection of the blessed life (*ultimus beatae vitae finis*). [3] The knowledge of God's judgment, wrath or vengeance certainly should not be called the knowledge of God, though it is a knowledge of His will. For the knowledge of God's will to be that knowledge of Him which is blessedness, it must be the knowledge of His *good*-will, His benevolence, towards us; that is, the knowledge of His mercy and kindness. Thus Calvin arrives at his definition of faith as knowledge: "that it is steadfast and sure knowledge of the Divine benevolence towards us, which, being founded on the truth of the gratuitous promise in Christ, is both revealed to our minds, and confirmed to our hearts, by the Holy Spirit". [4]

This "steadfast and sure knowledge", however, must not be regarded as a knowledge different from *the* knowledge of God the Creator and Redeemer. For the knowledge of the Creator and Redeemer consists in the knowledge of His will and especially of His benevolence—and this is Calvin's definition of faith. There is a sense, then, in which, although properly speaking faith precedes and leads to knowledge, yet it is itself the knowledge of God. To believe in God is to know God: the knowledge of God is a knowledge of faith. It is with this that we must now occupy

[1] *Inst.* I. x. 2. C.R. II, p. 73.
[2] *Inst.* III. ii. 6. C.R. II, p. 402.
[3] *Inst.* I. v. 1. C.R. II, p. 41.
[4] *Inst.* III. ii. 6. C.R. II, p. 402. Cf. *Le Catéchisme de Genève:* Faith is "certaine et ferme congnoissance de la dilection de Dieu envers nous." (C.R. VI, p. 43.)

H

ourselves. We have seen what is the object of the *cognitio Dei;* we must now seek to understand what Calvin means by knowledge and knowing.

The knowledge of God cannot be regarded as one of the branches of epistemology, but differs fundamentally from all other forms of knowing. This is not to deny the reality of the human activity which is involved in the expression "the knowledge of God". Man himself is the subject. But not only is the object of this knowledge different from the other objects of his knowledge; but because the object of this knowledge is God, whose difference from man is such that there exists a religious discontinuity between man and Him, the knowing itself is not of the same kind as those acts of knowing which have for their object something in the same dimension as man, and between which and his mind there exists therefore a likeness and a continuity. Knowing God is a unique activity in man's experience, having its own categories. It runs the risk, if it borrows from the categories of general epistemology, of destroying itself by turning its direction from its true object, God, to an idol fabricated by itself. For this reason (following Calvin) we cannot deal with knowledge either psychologically or philosophically, or rather we should say, that we cannot deal with knowledge according to the psychological or philosophical methods appropriate to the general branches of epistemology. Calvin approaches the knowledge of God by way of the knowledge of God in Jesus Christ by means of the Holy Spirit; and his concept of this knowledge is conditioned through and through by his insistence on the primacy and utter necessity of revelation.

In the first place, he conceived of the soul rather than of the mind as knowing: "Observe, that *the spirit of a man* is taken here for the soul in which the intellectual faculty, as it is called, resides. For Paul would have expressed himself inaccurately if he had ascribed this knowledge to man's intellect, or, in other words, to the faculty itself, and not to the soul, which is endued with the power of understanding". [1] In opposition to "the Philosophers" Calvin says that "the faculties of the soul consist in the mind and in the heart". [2] He will not allow the rigid division of man into

[1]*In I Cor.* 2. 11. C.R. XLIX, p. 342. C.T.S. I, p. 112.
[2]*Inst.* II. ii. 2. C.R. II, p. 186.

intellect, affection, senses, etc. This comes out in another context, when he is attacking the scholastic distinction between *fides informis* and *fides formata*. To allow that *fides informis* is a real faith, though needing to be "formed by love", is to separate arbitrarily the intellect from the soul. If, however, the intellect and the affections are the two "faculties of the soul", the one cannot be conceived of as active quite apart from the other without making the agent, not man, but a part of man. But for Calvin it is unthinkable that one part of man could be in a true relationship with God while another was totally unaffected by Him. Knowledge is the activity of the soul; that is, of the whole inward life of man. The knowledge of God, then, far from being a purely intellectual knowledge unrelated (or related only psychologically) to trust, reverence and love, is so closely bound up with these other forms of man's relationship to God as to be dependent upon them for its very being as real knowledge of God. Hence Calvin's insistence that true knowledge of the Creator is unthinkable apart from faith, fear and love. [1] Hence also, as we have seen, his denial of *fides informis*.

The knowledge of God resides in the soul's understanding. It is not, however, a knowledge which is arrived at by the mystical or rational activity, aided or unaided, of that understanding. For the object of knowledge being *super*natural, and cognition itself being natural, there must of necessity be that discontinuity between the object and the cognition that exists between natural and supernatural. Here Calvin differed decisively from the scholastic view that, as Professor Gilson puts it, man possesses "an intellect which is itself a participated likeness of the uncreated light in which dwell the Ideas". [2] The Fall, for the Thomists (although by making a closer connection between the nature of man and the *dona superaddita* than the Scotists, they were committed to holding that the loss of the one meant at least the impairing of the other) was not the irreparable cataclysm of human nature that it was for the Reformers. Whatever qualifications are made, the final Thomist word is that man's soul is wounded, not dead. "The work of creation is shattered, but the fragments remain good, and with the grace of God they may be

[1] *Inst.* I. ii.
[2] *The Spirit of Mediaeval Philosophy*, p. 140.

reconstituted and restored."[1] There is still, however we may safeguard it by insisting that *analogia entis* of necessity indicates unlikeness as well as likeness, a connection between man and God which is not one of grace and faith, but of being, and that conceived in such a way as to provide a starting-point that is not revelation but reason. Certainly St. Thomas never dreamed of laying the kingdom of Heaven open for man's unaided reason to grasp, but by allowing man's reason and the world of sensible things as starting-points for our knowledge of God, he to that extent minimises the revelation and the grace of God.

For Calvin, however, this knowledge is transcendent, quite above natural cognition. "When we call it knowledge, we intend not such a comprehension as men commonly have of those things which fall under the notice of their senses. For it is so superior, that the human mind must exceed and rise above itself, in order to attain to it."[2] "The reason why it is unknown is that it is too profound and sublime to be apprehended by the understanding of man. What a superior wisdom this is, which so far transcends all human understanding, that man cannot have so much as a taste of it!"[3] For this reason, what is needed, says Calvin, is a new mind that shall be able to understand: "There is an implied contrast between the spirit of our mind and the Divine and heavenly Spirit, who produces in us another and better mind".[4] "For, illuminated by Him [the Holy Spirit], the soul receives, as it were, new eyes for the contemplation of heavenly mysteries, by the splendour of which it was before dazzled."[5] This must not be taken literally, however. Calvin did not mean that our natural faculties are destroyed when we believe and new faculties given to us by the Spirit. He was no perfectionist. The "new and better mind" and the "new eyes" are to be taken as the illumination of the Holy Spirit; i.e. faith. It is indeed the human soul which knows God but it is the soul enlightened by the Holy Spirit. "It is only with the eye of faith that we can behold Him."[6]

[1] *The Spirit of Mediaeval Philosophy*, p. 127.
[2] *Inst.* III. ii. 14. C.R. II, p. 409.
[3] *In I Cor.* 2. 14. C.R. XLIX, p. 344. C.T.S. I, p. 116.
[4] *In Eph.* 4. 23. C.R. LI, p. 208. C.T.S., p. 295.
[5] *Inst.* III. ii. 34. C.R. II, p. 426.
[6] *In I Cor.* 1. 21. C.R. XLIX, p. 326. C.T.S. I, p. 85.

In other words, the knowledge of God is not a common act of cognition but the unique act of faith. It is man who knows, but his knowledge is faith—by virtue of the supernatural gift of God.

Whether Calvin held the *analogia entis* has been debated. Dr. Emil Brunner has asserted that he did.[1] Professor Lecerf, representative of classical Calvinism, treats it almost as a commonplace: "[Calvinism] knows, as well as its opponents, that men are 'the offspring of God' (Acts 17. 29), but it conceives this relationship as one of analogy, founded on the spiritual character of the human soul created in the image of God".[2] Two ideas in Calvin's thought lend their support to this. The first is his introduction of the innate *sensus deitatis* into the beginning of the *Institutio*. The second is the remnant of the *imago dei* which he allows that man possesses. We may rule out the fact that his concept of the knowledge of God is that it is analogical, for it has strictly nothing to do with the point at issue. All knowledge of God is analogical and sacramental, not direct. This is what revelation means. But it is axiomatic with the Reformers that the analogy must be chosen by God Himself to be the medium of His revelation. In this sense Jesus Christ, the Scriptures, preaching and the sacraments are analogies.

As for the *sensus deitatis*, we have already seen (and, in view of the very emphatic teaching of Inst. I. iv, it can hardly be denied) that it plays only the negative part of rendering man inexcusable for his sinful ignorance. For the second point, it must be at once confessed that Calvin does assert the relic of the *imago Dei:* "in the midst of the darkness, there are still some remains of light, which show in some degree the divine power of Christ".[3] "The divine image was not utterly annihilated and effaced."[4] We may also say that Calvin admits a certain likeness between the mind of man and the mind of God: "the mind of man is His true image";[5] "they have God present with them not only in the excellent gifts of the mind, but in their very essence";[6] "all mortal

[1]*Nature and Grace;* in *Natural Theology* (London, 1946), p. 55.
[2]*An Introduction to Reformed Dogmatics* (London, 1949), p. 286. Cf. pp. 21 and 97.
[3]*In Joann.* 1. 5. C.R. XLVII, p. 6. C.T.S. I, p. 33.
[4]*Inst.* I. xv. 4.
[5]*In Act.* 17. 22. C.R. XLVIII, p. 408. C.T.S. II, p. 154.
[6]*In Act.* 17. 28. C.R. XLVIII, p. 417. C.T.S. II, p. 169.

men are called sons in general, because they draw near to God in mind and understanding". [1]

But we must at once ask two questions: in what does this likeness consist? and, what use does Calvin make of it in the economy of salvation?

The bond between God and man consists, in the first place, in the subsistence of the life of man in God, the Fountain of life. This bond also exists, however, between God and all His creatures, inasmuch as He sustains them in life, and this life they have from Him. The peculiar link between God and man lies in the nature of man's life as differentiated from that of the brutes; that is, that he possesses an immortal soul and a rational understanding: "He speaks here, in my opinion, of that part of life in which men excel other animals; and informs us that the life which was bestowed on men was not of an ordinary description, but was united to the light of understanding". [2] The likeness between God and man, since it resides in the mind of man, is thus to be found in the relics of the *imago Dei*.

We must not yet say, however, that Calvin holds the *analogia entis* because he teaches a likeness between the mind of man and the mind of his Creator; for the expression *analogia entis* implies far more than this. It is invariably regarded as either an epistemological starting-point for the knowledge of God, or at least as a foundation on which God may build, and a point of contact between the Holy Spirit and man. We have already shown in Chapter Two, however, how Calvin always follows what appear to be generous concessions to natural theology by denying any religious validity to them at all. So it is here also. Calvin does not use this likeness between God and man in the way that Thomism and Calvinism do. The relics of the *imago Dei* which he regards man as unquestionably possessing are of no value for him in arriving at the knowledge of God beyond the obvious *sine qua non* that he is man, and it is to him as man that God's revelation is addressed. "*And the darkness did not comprehend it. Although by that small measure of light which still remains in us, the Son of God has always invited men to Himself, yet the Evangelist says that this was attended by no advantage, because

---

[1] *In Act.* 17. 28. C.R. XLVIII, p. 418. C.T.S. II, p. 170.
[2] *In Joann.* 1. 4. C.R. XLVII, p. 5. C.T.S. I, p, 32.

seeing, they did not see, (Matt. 13. 13). For since man lost the favour of God, his mind is so completely overwhelmed by the thraldom of ignorance, that any portion of light which remains in it is quenched and useless. This is daily proved by experience; for all who are not regenerated by the Spirit of God possess some reason . . . but by that guidance of their reason they do not come to God, and do not even approach to Him; so that all their understanding is nothing else than mere vanity. Hence it follows that there is no hope of the salvation of men, unless God grant new aid; for though the Son of God sheds His light upon them, they are so dull that they do not comprehend whence that light proceeds, but are carried away by foolish and wicked imaginations to absolute madness. . . . In short, natural reason will never direct men to Christ; and as to their being endued with prudence for regulating their lives, or being born to cultivate the liberal arts and sciences, all this passes away without yielding any advantage." [1]

To elucidate Calvin's thought here, we must turn once again to his passage on the understanding (*Institutio* II. ii. 12–21). What did man lose when he sinned? asks Calvin. Not his natural endowments, which distinguish him from the brutes, but those supernatural endowments which made him the image of God; that is, "the light of faith and righteousness, which would be sufficient for the attainment of a heavenly life and eternal felicity". [2] These were not inherent in his nature but were "ornaments" with which "he was decorated". Without them he would still be man, even though a ruined man. His natural endowments, however, he could not lose without ceasing to be man. At the Fall he lost his supernatural endowments, and his natural faculties, although not destroyed, were impaired: "soundness of mind and rectitude of heart were destroyed", [3] but not those faculties themselves. "Reason, therefore, by which man distinguishes between good and evil, by which he understands and judges, being a natural talent, could not be totally destroyed, but is partly debilitated, partly vitiated, so that it exhibits nothing but deformity and ruin." [4] In certain respects,

[1] *In Joann.* 1. 5. C.R. XLVII, pp. 6–7. C.T.S. I, pp. 33–4.
[2] *Inst.* II. ii. 12. C.R. II, p. 195.
[3] *Inst.* II. ii. 12. C.R. II, p. 195.
[4] *Inst.* II. ii. 12. C.R. II, p. 196.

however, the mind is capable; that is, in regard to what Calvin calls the *res terrenae*. [1] It can conceive and produce a *Summa Theologica*, a *Mass in B Minor*, a King's College Chapel, or a *Hamlet*. But it cannot break through into the realm of the mystery of God. As far as the *res coelestes* are concerned, "the wisest among men are blinder than moles". [2] "I call those things terrestial which do not pertain to God and His kingdom, to true righteousness, or to the blessedness of the future life; but which relate entirely to the present life, and are in some sense confined within the limits of it. Celestial things are the pure knowledge of God, the method of true righteousness, and the mysteries of the heavenly kingdom. In the first class are included civil polity, domestic economy, all the mechanical arts and liberal sciences. In the second, the knowledge of God and of the Divine will, and the rule for conformity to it in our lives." [3] Man is capable, to a greater or less degree according to his abilities, within the sphere of earthly things, but quite incapable in the heavenly realm. Therefore, what is needed is "a special illumination, not a common faculty of nature". [4] This illumination is the inward work of the Spirit, who "forms the ears to hear and the mind to understand". [5] "For in vain would the light present itself to the blind, unless the Spirit of understanding should open their mental eyes; so that He may be justly called the key with which the treasures of the kingdom of heaven are unlocked to us; and His illumination constitutes our mental eyes to behold them". [6] In other words, the gift of a new mind is the operation of the Holy Spirit changing what was unbelieving and also incapable of faith into a believing mind; not indeed into a mind

---

[1] Cf. Mr. P. S. Watson on Luther: "It is in virtue of his reason, Luther holds, that a man is worthy to be called, and is, a man. Reason is a 'natural light' that is kindled from the 'divine light', and 'above all other things of this life, it is something excellent and divine.' It is the discoverer and governor of all arts and sciences and 'whatever of wisdom, power, virtue, and glory is possessed by men in this life'. About reason in this sense of the term, Luther can wax almost lyrical. What he condemns is the use men commonly make of their reason, when they apprehend, judge, and discourse about matters pertaining to God and their own relationships with Him." (*Let God be God!* p. 86.)

[2] *Inst.* II. ii. 18. C.R. II, p. 200.

[3] *Inst.* II. ii. 13. C.R. II, p. 197.

[4] *Inst.* II. ii. 20. C.R. II, p. 201.

[5] *Inst.* II. ii. 20. C.R. II, p. 202.

[6] *Inst.* III. i. 4. C.R. II, p. 397. The 1560 French edition has the interesting variant: "*son illumination peut estre nommée La veue de nos ames.*" (C.R. IV, p. 7.)

capable of itself for believing and understanding, but a soul that is turned from itself to the wisdom of God in Jesus Christ. This orientation towards the Incarnate Son of God is the abdication of the sovereignty of reason and submission to the wisdom of God. It is repentance and faith. And as repentance is the humbling of the pride of the mind, so faith, built upon the "sight", the *notitia*, of Jesus of Nazareth, receives His witness concerning Himself, and knows God in Him as its Redeemer and Father.

Knowledge is no less real because it is the knowledge of faith. Indeed, according to Calvin it is stronger than natural cognition, which is subject to the variations of opinion incidental to human reasoning. But the knowledge of faith is peculiarly firm because it rests upon the promises of God which are true because God is true. The knowledge of God in Jesus Christ is, then, precisely because it is a transcendental knowledge, removed above the fluctuations of mortal existence. "To express the solid constancy of the persuasion, we further say, that it is a steadfast and sure knowledge. For as faith is not content with a dubious and versatile opinion, so neither with an obscure and perplexed conception; but requires a full and fixed certainty, such as is commonly obtained respecting things that have been tried and proved." [1] "In short, no man is truly a believer, unless he is firmly persuaded that God is a propitious and benevolent Father to him, and promises himself everything from His goodness; unless he depends on the promises of the Divine benevolence to him, and feels an undoubted expectation of salvation." [2] We have a real knowledge of God. In Jesus Christ, by the Holy Spirit, God really makes Himself known to us as the one who forgives our sins and quickens us to life in fellowship with Himself. Of this we are assured by the promises of God which are in Jesus Christ. And only so. For apart from Him we do not know God; if we do not rely upon Him we have no assurance of knowledge. "If you consider yourself, condemnation is certain; but since Christ, with all His benefits, is communicated to you, so that all that He has becomes yours, and you become a member of Him, and one with Him, His righteousness covers your sins;

[1] *Inst.* III. ii. 15. C.R. II, p. 410.
[2] *Inst.* III. ii. 16. C.R. II, p. 411.

His salvation supersedes your condemnation; He interposes with His merit, that your unworthiness may not appear in the Divine presence." [1]

Yet, although knowledge is real, it is not also perfect. It "consists more in certainty than in comprehension". [2] As revelation is always an indirect means of making known, so the knowledge of God is indirect. As He reveals to us *qualis sit erga nos* and not *quid sit*, so we always know Him in this life as He is towards us, and not as He is in Himself. This means that our knowledge is not, like other forms of knowledge, *sight*, but *faith*. Moreover, perfect assurance of faith does not exist in men —not because the object of faith is not assured, but because we are infirm and do not hold ourselves towards the object, but turn away to trust in ourselves or some other human agency. "When we teach that faith ought to be certain and secure, we conceive not a certainty attended with no doubt, or a security interrupted by no anxiety; but we rather affirm, that believers have a perpetual conflict with their own diffidence, and are far from placing their consciences in a placid calm, never disturbed by any storms. Yet, on the other hand, we deny that, however they may be afflicted, they ever fall and depart from that certain confidence which they have conceived in the Divine mercy." [3] Therefore he says elsewhere: "The knowledge of the godly is never so pure, but that some dimness or obscurity hangs over their spiritual vision". [4]

It is therefore necessary to increase in knowledge more and more. By continual study of the Scriptures, by life-long repentance, by discipline, by prayer, by all those practices of the Christian life which he enumerates in the third book of the *Institutio*, our knowledge of God becomes stronger in proportion as our ignorance is dispelled and our pride of mind is humbled. Yet this also is not a human achievement, although it is our duty to seek for God in His Word and to attempt to know Him by all the means that He has commanded. "For it is He who impresses His Word on our hearts by His Spirit, and it is He who daily chases away from our minds the clouds of ignorance which

[1] *Inst.* III. ii. 24. C.R. II, p. 418.
[2] *Inst.* III. ii. 14. C.R. II, p. 410.
[3] *Inst.* III. ii. 17. C.R. II, pp. 411-2.
[4] *In Eph.* 1. 16. C.R. LI, p. 155. C.T.S., p. 212.

obscure the brightness of the Gospel. In order that the truth may be fully revealed to us, we ought sincerely and earnestly to endeavour to attain it."[1] In the following passage is brought out very clearly the nature of knowledge as being real and assured and yet at the same time only partial:

"As soon as the smallest particle of grace is infused into our minds, we begin to contemplate the Divine countenance as now placid, serene and propitious to us: it is indeed a very distant prospect, but so clear that we know that we are not deceived. Afterwards, in proportion as we improve—for we ought to be continually improving by progressive advances—we arrive at a nearer, and therefore more certain view of Him, and by continual habit He becomes more familiar to us. Thus we see, that a mind illuminated by the knowledge of God, is at first involved in much ignorance, which is removed by slow degrees. Yet it is not prevented either by its ignorance of some things, or by its obscure view of what it beholds, from enjoying a clear knowledge of the Divine will respecting itself, which is the first and principal exercise of faith. For, as a man who is confined in a prison, into which the sun shines only obliquely and partially through a very small window, is deprived of a full view of that light, yet clearly perceives its splendour and experiences its beneficial influence; so we, who are bound with terrestial and corporeal fetters, though surrounded on all sides with great obscurity, are nevertheless illuminated sufficiently for all purposes of real security by the light of God shining, even though feebly, to reveal His mercy."[2]

Our knowledge of God is real but not perfect, and by the grace of God it increases more and more. But it is the knowledge of faith and therefore different from that knowledge which we shall enjoy hereafter. Revelation is indirect, we have said; knowledge is always by way of the sacramental form of

---

[1] *In Joann.* 8. 32. C.R. XLVII, p. 202. C.T.S. I, p. 341.
[2] *Inst.* III. ii. 19. C.R. II, pp. 413–4. Cf. *in Rom.* 1. 17, "When at first we taste the Gospel, we indeed see God's smiling countenance turned towards us, but at a distance. The more the knowledge of true religion grows in us, by coming as it were nearer we behold God's favour more clearly and more familiarly." C.R. XLIX, p. 21. C.T.S., p. 65. Also: "At that time they saw the glory of Christ, just as a man shut up in the dark obtains, through small chinks, a feeble and glimmering light. Christ now wishes that they shall make such progress as to enjoy the full brightness of heaven".—*In Joh.* 17. 24. C.R. XLVII, p. 389. C.T.S. II, p. 187.

revelation. We know God in His Word and in His works, because they are the image of God, mirroring His *effigies*, His portrait. "But then face to face: now I know in part; but then shall I know even as also I am known." "We, who have not as yet reached that great height, behold the image of God as it is presented before us in the Word, in the sacraments, in brief, in the whole service of the Church. . . . Our faith therefore at present beholds God as absent. How so? Because it sees not His face, but rests satisfied with the image in the mirror; but when we shall have left the world and gone to Him, it will behold Him as near and before its eyes. . . . Then we shall see God, not in His image, but in Himself."[1]

[1] *In* 1 *Cor.* 13. 12. C.R. XLIX, pp. 514–5. C.T.S. I, pp. 430–1.

APPENDIX

The Knowledge of God in Calvin's Theology by E. A. Dowey.
New York, 1952.

It never rains but it pours. No English work on this subject had
appeared until 1952, when within a few months of each other were
published Mr. Dowey's book and my own. Naturally, I read his
with lively interest, reviewing it in *The Evangelical Quarterly*. In
general, I was most impressed by its wide and detailed knowledge
of Calvin's writings and of books on Calvin, and there were, too,
many respects in which I found it illuminating. But I think that
anyone who reads the two works will agree with me that the most
striking fact about them lies in their disagreements. Starting from
the same evidence, they reach very different conclusions on one of
the principal issues—the place of the natural knowledge of God
in Calvin's thought. It is to this that I wish to narrow down our
present inquiry. But even on this chief point it is not necessary
to cover the whole ground; and therefore I have singled out as
vital the following: (i) The principle by which the *Institutio* is to
be interpreted. (ii) Mr. Dowey's conclusions on Calvin's use of
natural theology.

1

Apart from certain statements that if Calvin had been alive today
he would have gone to work differently—assertions easily made
on either side, but unhelpful in assessing his thought—Mr. Dowey
finds on more than one occasion that he has to alter the order of
the *Institutio*. The first concerns the form of the work as a whole.
Dowey, in agreement with Köstlin, considers the division of it
into four books as misleading,[1] and says that "the really significant
ordering principle of the *Institutes* in the 1559 edition is the
duplex cognitio Domini, not the Apostles' Creed".[2] Hence, he
would divide the *Institutio* into two parts: (1) Book I, on the
revelation and knowledge of the Creator; (2) Books II-IV, on the
revelation and knowledge of the Redeemer.[3]
Now we are here concerned with the difference between genuine

[1]pp. 41 ff.   [2]p. 42.   [3]p. 41.

and illegitimate textual criticism. It is illegitimate criticism to amend a passage or the order of passages against the author's avowed or known intention. We may disagree with that intention, but we cannot now change it, and therefore we have to conduct our criticism under its direction. With some writers it is difficult or impossible to arrive at their intention; but for the textual criticism of the *Institutio* we are happily situated, for not only is there no doubt that the 1559 edition was arranged by Calvin himself, but also that he was quite satisfied with it and did not contemplate any further revision.[1] Therefore, although there is nothing to prevent us criticising the form as clumsy or inadequate, we are not at liberty to change it into another form altogether and then discuss the result as if we were still discussing Calvin. But this is just what Dowey does.

He seems to think that we are faced with the alternatives of grouping Books I-III together, with their Trinitarian titles, leaving Book IV outside, or of making Book I a kind of introduction to the rest, "setting the context and proposing the categories within which the latter is to be grasped".[2] But the fourfold ordering of the Apostles' Creed need cause us no embarrassment. It was Calvin's custom from the beginning to divide it in this way, as we see from the 1536 *Institutio*[3] or from *Le Catechisme de l'Eglise de Geneve*, whose third section begins roundly with the question: "To explain this confession of faith in detail, how many parts do we divide it into? *Answer*: Into four heads."[4] In 1559, therefore, he was merely following his customary order.

But this is not Dowey's primary problem, and he can speak of "the excellence and even beauty of Calvin's final arrangement in terms of the creed".[5] He rearranges the *Institutio* because he regards it as a dissertation on the *duplex cognitio Domini*, the knowledge of the Creator and the knowledge of the Redeemer, which is not brought out sufficiently clearly by Calvin's own ordering: "Calvin's final plan, which from the epistemological view follows the *duplex cognitio* and not the Creed, is simply the systematic arrangement most compatible with his concept of the knowledge of God."[6]

[1]*Inst.*; To the Reader: "I was never satisfied, until it was arranged in the order in which it is now published."
[2]p. 41. [3]Op. sel. I. pp. 75-93. [4]Op. sel. II. p. 76.
[5]p. 42, n.4. [6]p. 49.

Now if the *Institutio* did revolve around the *duplex cognitio Domino*, a twofold arrangement would be most convenient. But the excellence and beauty of the *Institutio* (to take up Dowey's words) consists formally in its unity, a unity that Calvin was striving towards in the earlier editions. To impose upon it the *duplex cognitio Dei* is to destroy that unity and to make it such a badly arranged book that we should be very surprised that a theologian of Calvin's taste should have professed himself satisfied with it.

We may say, however, that the *Institutio* does in fact reflect a *duplex cognitio*; but the *cognitio* is the knowledge of God and of ourselves, a concept that opens every edition "Wellnigh the whole sum of our wisdom *duabus partibus constat, Dei cognitione et nostri*". It is in this way that the editors of the Amsterdam edition interpret the matter: "The author has a double aim in this Christian Institute: the former, the knowledge of God, by which we reach blessed immortality. The latter is the knowledge of ourselves, determined to that first."[1] Such a reading comes out of Calvin's expressed intention, preserves the unity of the *Institutio* and requires no re-ordering of the material to justify it.

Hence the theme of the *Institutio* may be stated as follows: The two parts of wisdom, the knowledge of God and of ourselves, are closely interwoven; so closely, indeed, that Calvin cannot treat of the one without the other throughout the whole work. The two themes continue side by side and only for convenience in arrangement will he temporarily lay aside the one or the other. As soon as he has established this *duplex cognitio*, he says: "But though the knowledge of God and the knowledge of ourselves be intimately connected, the proper order of teaching requires us first to treat of the former and then to proceed to the discussion of the latter."[2] He therefore goes on to the knowledge of God, of the God who is our Creator, Redeemer and Sanctifier. This entails at once a further distinction—the *duplex cognitio Domino*. And this also is a matter of arrangement: "a twofold knowledge of Him, of which the former is first to be treated now, and then the other will follow *suo ordine*".[3] The same God is our Creator and Redeemer. If we are to know God, we must know Him as Creator

---

[1]*Inst. Chr. Relig. methodus & dispositio*, quoted from Elzevir edition, 1654.
[2]*Inst.* I. i. 3.   [3]*Inst.* I. ii. 1.

and Redeemer—and correspondingly, to describe the knowledge of God, Calvin must describe it as a knowledge of the Creator and Redeemer. The rest of Book I tells us that we fail to know God through the creation, but that in the Scriptures He reveals Himself as the Creator.

Book II, on the Knowledge of God the Redeemer, begins with five chapters on the knowledge of ourselves. These are not, as Dowey supposes,[1] out of place here, so that Book II should properly begin with Chapter vi. Nor are we taking "a whole new orientation" or jumping to "another starting point theologically".[2] We are still concerned with the knowledge of God and of ourselves; our Creator is our Redeemer and we creatures are sinners. Indeed, Calvin is very careful to relate these two aspects: "But the knowledge of ourselves consists first, in considering what was bestowed on us at our creation, and the favours we continually receive from the Divine goodness, that we may know how great the excellence of our nature would have been, if it had retained its integrity; . . . Secondly, we should contemplate our miserable condition since the fall of Adam, the sense of which tends to destroy all boasting and confidence, to overwhelm us with shame and to fill us with real humility."[3] Book II leads on from Book I; but we shall understand this only if we grasp the unity of Calvin's purpose of describing the relationship between God and man.

The same theme is continued in Book III, where the objectivity of the previous book is transmuted into subjectivity, *Christus pro nobis* into *Christus in nobis* through His Holy Spirit. Epistemologically, this book deals with man's knowing of God the Creator and Redeemer in Christ through the enlightening of the Holy Spirit. Plainly, in accordance with the title the substance of the book will be predominantly concerned with redemption. But not to the exclusion of the fact that God is also our Creator. We may instance III.x: "The Right Use of the Present Life", where Calvin again turns to the theme of creation, or III.xx, where he thinks of prayer in reference to man as God's redeemed creature, who in Jesus Christ may call upon his Creator for all his earthly needs, or III.xxi-xxiv, but especially xxiii, where in his discussion of predestination Calvin very obviously has in mind God who is Creator and Redeemer and man as His reprobate or elect creature.

[1] p. 45.   [2] p. 147.   [3] *Inst.* II. i. 1.

Book III carries on into Book IV with its insistence that this work of the Holy Spirit takes place through *externa media*, within the Church and by means of those external ordinances that Christ has ordained.

We may conclude, then, that the *Institutio* is not to be divided arbitrarily into a form that Calvin did not give it. The form that Dowey imposes on it does not correspond to the general theme, but takes one methodological distinction made in the work and magnifies it into the leading principle to interpret the whole. In this way an independent place can be given to the doctrine of the knowledge of the Creator and Book I made into a sort of prolegomena to the rest, "setting the context and proposing the categories, within which the latter is to be grasped".[1] Classical Calvinism and nineteenth and twentieth century dogmatics followed that course with their custom of beginning with a section on the philosophy of religion. Calvin knew better. It is highly significant that Dowey has to have a final chapter entitled *The Relation between the Knowledge of God the Creator and the Knowledge of God the Redeemer*.[2] Obviously, positing a *duplex cognitio Domini* as the heart of a theology, such a relating and reconciling is necessary. Calvin himself not only did not have this sort of relating to do, but he did not need to, for the *duplex cognitio Domini Creatoris et Redemptoris* was not the theme of the *Institutio*.

2

As we turn to Calvin's use of the word *inexcusability*, we must explain why we single out this particular point. In spite of the misinterpretation of the *Institutio* that we have just considered, Dowey certainly does not make Calvin contradict himself and become a straightforward "natural theologian". Indeed, he quotes the passages where Calvin denies the validity of the knowledge gained apart from the Scriptures. But he will nevertheless give it a too positive function and thus carry over such knowledge as a valuable component of Christian preaching. It is because this concept of inexcusability is the heart of the matter here that we have to try to understand what Calvin meant by it and in what way he uses it.

Inexusabilis is the common translation, used also by Calvin, for

[1] p. 41.   [2] pp. 221 ff.

ἀναπολόγητος a word which occurs twice in the New Testament, in Romans 1:20: "For the invisible things of him since the creation of the world are clearly seen, being perceived through the things that are made, even his everlasting power and divinity; εἰς τὸ εἶναι αὐτοὺς ἀναπολογήτους—ut sint inexcusabiles", and in Romans 2:1: "Wherefore thou art ἀναπολόγητος—inexcusabilis— O man, whosoever thou art that judgest." The noun ἀπολογία comes more frequently, in the sense of a speech made by a prisoner in his own defence, mostly in justification of his actions rather than denial of them. (E.g. in Acts 22:1, 25:16, 1 Cor. 9:3, 2 Cor. 7:11.) Ἀναπολόγητος taken literally will therefore mean that the prisoner has no ἀπολογία to offer.

Calvin takes up this word and uses it very frequently, especially in the context of natural theology. We may see first what he makes of it in his exposition of Romans 1:20. God's manifestation of Himself in the creation is clear enough to lead to a knowledge of Him. It is, however, insufficient in that we are blind to it. Yet we are not so blind that we cannot conceive that it is related to something divine whom we deduce should be worshipped (Concipimus divinitatem: deinde eam quaecunque est, colendam esse ratiocinamur). We go no further than this and do not know who this divinity is or what He is like (aut quis, aut qualis sit Deus). The knowledge that there is a God who should be worshipped leads to no positive relationship to God "but serves only to take away excuse". Inexcusability means, therefore, "that men can plead no defence at the judgment of God to show that they are not rightly to be condemned (iure damnabiles)".

The same argument comes in the crucial passage in the Institutio which sets a sign of negation against the possibility of a natural knowledge of God. In line with Romans 1 (and the importance of that chapter could hardly be overestimated in the formation of the beginning of the Institutio) Calvin says: "The invisible Deity was represented by such visible objects (spectaculis), yet we have no eyes to see Him except they be enlightened through faith by an inward revelation of God."[1] And then, with direct reference to Romans 1:20, he goes on that Paul does not "intend such a manifestation as human perspicacity may comprehend, but rather shows that its utmost extent is to make men inexcusabiles".[2] He

[1] Inst. I. v. 14.   [2] Ibid.

again gives, in effect, an explanation of *inexcusabilis*: A defect in
ourselves prevents us from making the proper use of the revelation
in the creation, and as this defect is our own fault we are left without any evasion (*tergiversatio*). We cannot plead ignorance, for
dumb creatures proclaim the truth, eyeless creatures demonstrate
it and irrational creatures teach it—"all things show us the right
way". Hence, "we are justly excluded from all excuse".[1]

From this the colouring that *inexcusabilis* had for Calvin becomes clear. It bears the forensic significance of an accused
person pleading some justification for his actions before his Divine
Judge. One by one the excuses as to why he did not know, love
and serve God are swept away until he can only plead ignorance
in that the Gospel had never been preached to him and he had
never even heard of Christ. But even this will not avail, for his
Judge points him to the creation where He was clearly to be seen
and then the accused is *inexcusabilis*, ἀναπολόγητος, with nothing
to say for himself, no reason to plead why the just condemnation
should not be executed.

Hence, the revelation in the creation has only a negative function
apart from the self-revelation of God as the Creator in the Scriptures. When God reveals Himself there, man sees that the
universe is the Creation of God and history the scene of His
providence. It is in this way that Calvin himself will preach on,
for example, Job 38 ff. Preaching within the sphere of the Church
and to those who, even if they are not believers, are nevertheless
familiar with the message of the Gospel, Calvin looks at the
creation with the spectacles of Scripture firmly before his eyes and
sees and points out the Creator and Lord of history. In such a
situation the negative function plays only a small part. Rather, he
insists that the *opera dei* in creation and history should fill us with
wonder and praise and prostrate us in humility before God.

Where I dissent from Dowey is that I do not think he gives
sufficient weight to the concept of inexcusability in the sense in
which we have regarded it above. He concentrates on Calvin's
expositions of Acts 14 and 17 in an attempt to reinstate the concept in a more positive role and to find in Calvin the germ of an
"eristics". His summary runs as follows: "The man of faith, then,
who knows from the word the inexcusability of mankind, can

[1] *Inst.* I. v. 15.

bring that consciousness to the pagan unbeliever by argumentation based on the revelation in creation. This does not lead directly to faith, but to awareness of the insufficiency of this or that heathen creed. After this, the gospel is introduced."[1]

This second sentence is applicable as the programme of a modern apologist, but it rings quite false of Calvin. "Insufficiency" is far too weak to describe his attitude to the non-Christian religions. He regarded man outside Christ as ungodly, perverted and malicious in outlook and utterly wrong-thinking and his religion as false and worthless. Hence, he did not envisage Paul proving from nature that the men of Lystra and Athens had an insufficient religion which needed to be changed for another or perhaps filled up and made sufficient or that he was first "clearing away the bad" to make room for the good; but he saw him telling the hearers that in the sight of God they were guilty sinners with nothing to plead in self-defence, not even ignorance, since, if they had not been blind through their malice, they would have known Him by the light He affords in nature. They are *inexcusabiles*. Their one hope is not to delude themselves with vain attempts to find some excuse in the end, but to accept the position—i.e. to repent.

Moreover, in the passage quoted, Dowey under-estimates a vital factor in Calvin's view of Acts 14 and 17. This is not at all an instance of man perceiving the revelation in creation and providence *per se*, but of that same revelation seen through the spectacles of the Scriptures. Not only is there no question of the heathen hearers arriving at an awareness of inexcusability by their own reading of creation, but neither are the preachers speaking as natural men. Speaking as they have been taught by the Scriptures, they declare that the Creator and Provider of all things is the God of the Bible. In a quotation from the Commentary on Acts 17, Dowey emphasizes a clause that would make it seem as if the apostles were speaking by the light of nature: "*men cannot be led to a saving knowledge of God except by the direction of the word. And yet this does not prevent but that they may be made inexcusable without the word . . .*"[2] But "without the word" in this context merely means "without direct reference to the Scriptures", or in Calvin's own words, "There is no direct mention made of the

[1] p. 86.   [2] p. 85 (Dowey's italics).

Word." For we cannot possibly imagine that Calvin is allowing to the apostles in this instance a perception that he continually denies elsewhere—that they were seeing and commenting on the revelation in creation with their own unaided eyesight. If in fact they were speaking of it as they had been taught by the Scriptures, they were speaking *with* the Word in substance, *without* the Word only inasmuch as they neither quoted nor referred to the Bible.

To sum up, then, the only "apologetic" use that Calvin allows to the revelation in creation is a very different one from what modern apologetics see as its task. There is no question of its providing a stepping-stone towards the truth, of its proving a foundation to build on. In itself, apart from the Scriptures, it has merely made every man objectively inexcusable before God, i.e. whether he knows it or not, his excuses are in fact invalid in God's eyes. In itself, it cannot do more than this; nor has any man the ability of himself to make himself or his neighbour aware of his inexcusability by means of it. When it is understood in the light of Scripture, it still possesses a negative value only, or we might, in analogy to the Law, call it a killing or wounding function in opposition to the quickening and healing office of the Gospel— the preacher declares to the heathen that they have no excuse for not knowing, loving and serving God and therefore are justly liable to eternal death. If they recognize and acknowledge their inexcusability they are repenting and if they repent they will be pointed to Christ and faith in Him.

There can be no doubt that Calvin must be cleared of any charge of being a natural theologian, or of having an "apologetic" programme. The only point on which he can be regarded as guilty in this respect is that he does not make it clear that Christ is the starting point for all understanding of God, whether as Redeemer or as Creator. That he himself believed this can be proved a thousand times from his writings; but in the *Institutio* he did not apply it sufficiently strictly in the early chapters, with the result that he can be misinterpreted as a natural theologian. In fact, however, the worst that he can be found guilty of is inconsistency; and it is not difficult to correct his inconsistency from the abundant evidence of his essential attitude throughout all his works.

WORKS OF CALVIN QUOTED

Christianae Religionis Institutio. Basileae. 1536. (C.R. I.)
Institutio Christianae Religionis. Argentorati. 1539. (C.R. I.)
Institutio Christianae Religionis. Genevae. 1559. (C.R. II.)
Institution de la Religion Chrestienne. Geneve. 1541. (C.R. III–IV.)
Institution de la Religion Chrestienne. A Geneve. 1560. (C.R. III-IV.)
Petit Traicté de la Saincte Cene. A Geneve. 1541. (C.R. V.)
Le Catéchisme de l'Eglise de Genève. A Geneve. 1545. (C.R. VI.)

COMMENTARIES:

Genesis.	1554.	(C.R. XXIII.)
Psalms.	1557.	(C.R. XXXI–XXXII.)
Isaiah.	1559.	(C.R. XXXVI–XXXVII.)
Harmony of the Gospels.	1555.	(C.R. XLV.)
John.	1553.	(C.R. XLVII.)
Acts.	1552–54.	(C.R. XLVIII.)
Romans.	1540.	(C.R. XLIX.)
I Corinthians.	1546.	(C.R. XLIX.)
Galatians.	1548.	(C.R. L.)
Ephesians.	1548.	(C.R. LI.)
Philippians.	1548.	(C.R. LII.)
Colossians.	1548.	(C.R. LII.)
I Timothy.	1548.	(C.R. LII.)
I John.	1551.	(C.R. LV.)

SERMONS:

On Deuteronomy.
   (Preached 1555–6.) (C.R. XXV–XXIX.)
On Harmony of Gospels.
   (Preached 1559–64.) (C.R. XLVI.)

LIST OF BOOKS QUOTED

C. F. Andrews: *What I Owe to Christ.*
S. Thomas Aquinas: *Summa Theologica.*
S. Athanasius: *De Incarnatione.*
S. Augustine: *In Joannis Evangelium tractatus.*
Karl Barth: *Die Kirchliche Dogmatik* I. 1.
Karl Barth: *Die Kirchliche Dogmatik* II. 1.
Karl Barth: *The Knowledge of God and the Service of God.*
Karl Barth: *Credo.*
Karl Barth: *Nein!*
Peter Barth: *The Biblical Basis of Calvin's Doctrine of Predestination* (in *De l'Election Eternelle de Dieu*).
Peter Barth: *Das Problem der natürlichen Theologie bei Calvin.*
J. Bossuet: *De la connoissance de Dieu et de soi-même.*
E. Brunner: *The Mediator.*
E. Brunner: *Revelation and Reason.*
E. Brunner: *The Word and the World.*
E. Brunner: *Nature and Grace.*
R. Bultmann: *Jesus and the Word.*
J. Burnaby: *Amor Dei.*
G. K. Chesterton: *St. Francis of Assisi.*
Clement of Alexandria: *Stromata.*
Cyril of Jerusalem: *Catechetical Lectures.*
A. Dakin: *Calvinism.*
R. E. Davies: *The Problem of Authority in the Continental Reformers.*
G. P. Fisher: *History of Christian Doctrine.*
E. Gilson: *The Spirit of Mediaeval Philosophy.*
E. Gilson: *The Philosophy of St. Bonaventure.*
T. R. Glover: *The Jesus of History.*
G. S. Hendry: *God the Creator.*
S. Hilary: *De Trinitate.*
K. Holl: *Johannes Calvin.*
W. R. Inge: Art. *Logos* in *H.E.R.E.*
R. Jefferies: *The Story of My Heart.*
A. Lecerf: *An Introduction to Reformed Dogmatics.*
Luther: *Introduction to O.T.*
Luther: *Commentary on Genesis.*
Luther: *Commentary on Galatians.*
Luther: *Die drei Symbola.*
Luther: *Letter to Georg Spenlein.*
J. W. Marmelstein: *Étude comparative des Textes latins et francais de l'Institution de la Religion Chrestienne par Jean Calvin.*
P. Melanchthon: *Loci Communes.* 1521.
J. Oman: *Honest Religion.*
W. Temple: *Nature, Man and God.*

B. B. Warfield: *Calvin and Calvinism.*
P. S. Watson: *Let God be God!*
N. P. Williams: *The Ideas of the Fall and of Original Sin.*
H. Zwingli: *Werke.* 1828. Bd. I.

The following books, not quoted in this essay, are the most important among a good number that helped me with an understanding of the general background of the subject:

J. Baillie: *Our Knowledge of God.* (London, 1939.)
H. Bavinck: *The Philosophy of Revelation.* (New York, 1909.)
E. Brunner: *Man in Revolt.* (London, 1939.)
J. Butler: *The Analogy of Religion* . . . (ed. J. H. Bernard. London. 1900.)
E. Gilson: *The Philosophy of St. Thomas.* (Cambridge, 1929.)
E. Gilson: *The Mystical Theology of St. Bernard.* (London, 1940.)
H. M. Gwatkin: *The Knowledge of God.* (London, 1906.)
W. R. Inge: *Christian Mysticism.* (1921.)
H. L. Mansel: *The Limits of Religious Thought.* (London, 1858.)
H. Wheeler Robinson: *Redemption and Revelation.* (London, 1943.)
R. Seeberg: *Dogmengeschichte* III. pp. 568–92. (On Duns Scotus.)

INDEX OF NAMES

www.ingramcontent.com/pod-product-compliance
Lightning Source LLC
Chambersburg PA
CBHW071811090426
42737CB00012B/2046